D0463552

The Cradle of *Erewhon*

Samuel Butler in New Zealand

Samuel Butler: Christchurch, 1862

The Cradle of
Erewhon

Samuel Butler in New Zealand

By JOSEPH JONES

AUSTIN . UNIVERSITY OF TEXAS PRESS

Library of Congress Catalog Card No. 59–8125

© 1959 by the University of Texas Press

Manufactured in the United States of America
by the Printing Division of the University of Texas

TO MANY FRIENDS IN NEW ZEALAND:

Kia ora!

Preface and Acknowledgments

Exactly a hundred years ago Samuel Butler set out on an adventure that was to prove the most dramatic gesture of his life: emigration to New Zealand, offering asylum at the other end of the earth from a tangle of domestic difficulty. This "exile" lasted five years, and out of it came that curious blending of candor and enigma, sense and perversity, called *Erewhon*. Had Butler stayed home there would have been no *Erewhon* and the world would lack one of its great satires. It would seem, therefore, that rather close attention should have been paid the milieu out of which so remarkable a book emerged.

New Zealand, notwithstanding its obvious bearing upon Butler and his books, has received less notice than it deserves. The circumstance of distance has kept most Butlerians from seeing for themselves what the country is really like; and their efforts to use the evidence procurable through reading and correspondence have not been as thorough as was needful. Harkness' assiduous and generally comprehensive bibliography of Butler (1955), for example, manages to overlook John Pascoe's considerable comment on Butler in his books on New Zealand mountaineering, not to mention A. C. Brassington, M. H. Holcroft, Oliver Duff, and some other New Zealanders who have had something or other to say about Butler. A recent book on Darwin and Huxley places Butler's sheep farming in Australia! And so it goes. The present work, based on study and travel in New Zealand made possible through a Fulbright lectureship some five years ago, is an effort to interpret more adequately than has hitherto been done the meaning that New Zealand had for Butler's life and work.

Occasionally the matter of Butler's pioneering sojourn has come up for brief attention. H. J. Massingham, writing in the *Geographical Magazine* in 1936, points out that "Butler is one of the very few men in English literary history whose body and mind, each in its own sphere of action, undertook the adventure perilous in the discovery of new lands." Massingham also has some perceptive things to say about *A First Year in Canterbury Settlement*, noting Butler's virulent prejudice against it and remarking that "the book's readers will never see eye to eye with him." I have attempted, with the help of some hitherto unnoticed critical opinion of *A First Year*, to explore a little into the reasons for Butler's rejection of the work.

The rejection of *A First Year*, however, may be only symbolic of Butler's attempt to reject his colonial experience *in toto*. This suggests in turn a large and admittedly debatable question: what was the final cost of such rejection? In arguing that it may have been more than Butler ever realized or would have been willing to concede, I hope I have been able to muster enough evidence to make the matter at least worth considering, though I am aware that whoever meddles with Butler is likely to start more hares than he can chase.

I have not dealt with Butler's afterfame in New Zealand except incidentally. It is to be hoped that someone on the ground may undertake the considerable task of rounding up the miscellaneous Butleriana that must still exist there, with the aim of studying definitively Butler's reputation in the land that had so much to do with his entry into the world of letters.

My obligations to a host of people in New Zealand are implied, to a degree, in the Dedication. I am indebted especially to the Alexander Turnbull Library and the General Assembly Library of Wellington, to the Auckland Public Library, the Canterbury Museum and the Robert McDougall Art Gallery of Christchurch, to W. S. Baverstock, A. C. Brassington, A. B. Cochran, Ian Gordon, E. H. McCormick, S. Morrison, S. Musgrove, John Pascoe, Mr. and Mrs. M. Prouting (present owners of Mesopotamia Station), R. T. Robertson, and C. R. H. Taylor. The assistance of Miss Kathleen Blow of The University of Texas Library has been invaluable on numerous occasions. A grant from the University Research Institute provided secretarial service, rendered most ably by Mrs. Robert D. Turpin.

Acknowledgment is made to the Caxton Press, Christchurch, for permission to quote passages from the poems of A. R. D. Fairburn and Denis Glover.

To my wife, son, and daughters, who went with me to "Ao Tea Roa" in 1953, I hope this book may recall enough pleasant memories to obscure some of the tribulations which those nearest a seat of authorship must inevitably share.

J. J.

September, 1958
Austin, Texas

Contents

Illustrations

Photographs

Part I: Mesopotamian Squatter

'*Observe the young and tender frond*
'*of this punga: shaped and curved*
'*like the scroll of a fiddle: fit instrument*
'*to play archaic tunes.*'
                    '*I see*
'*the shape of a coiled spring.*'

A. R. D. FAIRBURN

YOUNG BUTLER:
Emigration or Frustration?

*For young men, however, sons of gentlemen and
gentlemen themselves, sheep or cattle are the most
obvious and best investment.*

A FIRST YEAR IN CANTERBURY SETTLEMENT

In 1851 gold was discovered in Australia. The discovery came not a
moment too soon. Overpopulation in England—part of the price of
frenetic industrialization—was begetting industrial poverty with more
than enough political and social uneasiness to make emigration popular both to the governed and their governors. Rapidly the stigma of
"Botany Bay" faded into folklore as Englishmen of all callings and
classes took ship first for Melbourne and only a little later for Sydney,
cities which mushroomed at a rate to rival San Francisco and Chicago.
The great American directive of the nineteenth century, "Go west,
young man, and grow up with the country," had been uttered the same
year—a date thus full of meaning for English-speaking pioneers,
whether British or American.

But in "Go *south,* young man . . ." the corollary of growing up with
the country was not always in the minds of the emigrants. For generations India had been the lure for the get-rich-quick, and it was natural

3

enough to suppose that the other colonies might be similarly open to exploitation. How many of the gold-seekers intended more than a year or so of roughing it, to be followed by a lifetime of gentlemanly repose at home, cannot be known with certainty, but in all probability the majority nursed some such illusion. Many left their bones in the diggings; many more became permanent settlers; some few came home with well-lined pockets.

The magnetic pull of the gold fields, at any rate, was indisputable. Viewing with alarm the eagerness of Englishmen to lose their head in a gold rush as precipitately as the American forty-niners, the *Illustrated London News* in an editorial of May 22, 1852, attempted to sober its readers by reminding them that gold rushing is always a lottery:

We shall, no doubt, have to record, after the lapse of a certain time, that the old experiences have been repeated—that countless bubbles have risen, floated, and glittered in the sunshine, that they have been borne aloft for the credulous to admire, and that they have collapsed with the customary results, bitter regrets expressed too late, and the misery if not the ruin of thousands of people.

Granting that the accession of so much new wealth might ultimately prove to be politically of great significance, the *News* was still shocked. Word had come that everybody in Australia was off to the mines:

that the sheep remain unshorn, that an amount of property in wool alone worth far more than all the gold yet obtained has been lost to the colonies, and that, unless a large supply of men, women, and children be immediately sent out, and be followed at regular intervals by other supplies as large and continuous, the noblest colony ever possessed by any empire, and one of the noblest countries in the world, will be totally ruined, notwithstanding its gold.

Australia as "one of the noblest countries in the world" was something of a new note. Perhaps in his excitement the editor had said more than he intended, but at least Australia was better than California:

4

California has no treasure but its gold; but Australia possesses that which is better than gold, and of which gold is but the arithmetical gauge and measurement:—It possesses flocks and herds in countless abundance; it grows corn, and wine, and fruit; and produces every article necessary for the subsistence, the health, the comfort, and even for the luxury of man. It has a fine soil, a splendid climate, harbours and rivers, and every natural advantage to make it the seat of one of the most powerful empires that ever existed on the globe. But it has one great want—that of human arms. It needs but men to possess wealth sufficient to buy up a score of barren and pestilential Californias, and to become a Southern Britain, richer, and possibly happier than its mother-land. But its gold fields, with their glittering prizes, by discovery of which men hope to gain, and very many do gain, rapid fortunes in periods of time that to our sober judgments on this side of the world look incredibly short, appear to be destroying a far truer and more valuable source of wealth than mere unsupported gold can ever become.

All this exhortation, naturally, fell on deaf ears, but the moral contained a germ of truth that had already begun to prove itself. Fortunes *were* to be made in the Antipodes by means other than digging and sluicing. The Australian sheep rancher, or "squatter," was becoming a person of consequence—not yet a nabob, perhaps, but still somebody substantial enough to make his influence felt in the colony and in a few instances to show himself in England. When the gold fever subsided, there would be more of him than ever, with prosperous cities to handle his goods, do his banking, and provide him very nearly all the comforts of "Home," short of nightingales and the view of St. Paul's from the Thames. The *Illustrated London News* was right; there was plenty to be had from the land, if one had a bit of initial capital and plenty of stamina to force the land to yield.

What the *News* had said of Australia was applicable on a smaller scale, but in general a more sedate and comfortable scale, to New Zealand. The "flocks and herds in countless abundance" were already being introduced there, and in most parts of the two islands the "fine soils, splendid climate, harbours and rivers, and every natural advantage" were potentially equal to those of Australia, or the parts of Australia, that is, which were then receiving attention. Though politically independent of each other and culturally quite disparate, the two colonies were near enough neighbors to offer the emigrant an easy alternative. Many early colonists arrived in New Zealand only after having sojourned in Australia, rather than coming directly out from "Home."

Samuel Butler was sixteen when all this began to happen. It would be another decade before he was ready for the plunge himself—a decade during which he was building up enough antagonisms to make emigration the natural, the all but inevitable, solution to his difficulties. Quite possibly, looking at it from another direction, the prospects of success attending emigration may have had something to do with creating in Butler, and numerous other independently-minded young men, the courage to think seriously of breaking away for themselves. The safety valve was available, and looking better every year.

For young Sam, however, the normal lure of emigration was less insistent than a mounting sense of special personal crisis. Gradually but most insidiously, he came to feel, he had been victimized by a clergyman father—inveigled into preparing himself for the church before he was intellectually in position to square off and examine the church for what it was. It has been a matter of some debate whether the father, the Rev. Thomas Butler, canon of Langar, was culpable to the degree later charged by the son in his conversation, his letters, and most notably *The Way of All Flesh,* published posthumously in 1903. Most of the surviving documents are prejudicial either in content or intention—the series of selected and carefully posed biographical "remains" rather more so than the comparatively judicious though certainly not compassionate overtones of the autobiographical novel (which was finished about 1884, nearly a score of years before Butler's death in 1902). For better or worse, the average reader takes *The Way of All Flesh* as a symbolic representation of Butler's own personal difficulties; and there seems no very real doubt that it was so intended. What were the actualities?

Butler's childhood, we judge, had been scarcely less ill-starred than Dickens' or Byron's. To one less sensitive, one better geared to the cast-iron paternalism of the day, the shelter of a well-to-do rectory, coupled with the promise of a solid education and easy entry into a highly respected profession, would have been easy enough to accept. But not for Samuel Butler, or for that matter for his younger brother Tom, who pleased his parents even less than the elder son. Butler endured his schooling more than he enjoyed it until he entered St. John's College, Cambridge, where he began to sense the possibility of liberation.

Out of college at twenty-three, demanding the young man's perennial demand to live his own life, Butler rejected the church and was drawn strongly toward music and painting. A wanderer within reasonable (hardly Odyssean) bounds, he had come also to relish Continental ways of life, in Italy especially and in the Alps. But the life of the artist, of all possible choices, Thomas Butler could not accept for his son. In the ensuing quarrel, or series of quarrels, Samuel demanded his share of the substantial inheritance ultimately due him from his grandfather's estate. Believing that emigration was at least preferable to bohemianism at home, Canon Butler agreed to finance a venture to some one of the expanding settlements in numerous parts of the British Empire. New Zealand, for prudential and on the whole quite adequate and sensible reasons, was the place at length agreed upon. Five years, from 1859 to 1864, turned out to be the term of exile—or of opportunity, depending on how one views the matter.

What were these five years to mean, years which in pioneering countries have a way of compressing experience into small but weighty and efficient packages (as Butler learned to compress his own wool bales) and forcing maturity upon young men? Was he to be the same difficult sort of personality in the colony, or would so antithetic a gesture prove extreme enough to calm him down, to content him for a time?

By taking residence in New Zealand, Butler would seem to have intended widening the breach with his family: he would do anything and everything physically possible to make sure of the separation he

7

felt was so needful. But if he really hated them so much, why—once well away—should he have returned? This is by no means an easy question to answer, but an examination of the circumstances of his life in the colony may make it at any rate an easier question to ask and at the same time one better worth the asking.

"He grew up under Victorianism, he was nearly strangled by it and had to fight against it," says E. M. Forster, "and only saved his soul by escaping to New Zealand."[1] If he did actually save his soul—or, as he himself phrased it, stole his birthright—there must have been more to it than the bare achievement of escaping. Escape he did; in what special ways, if any, was New Zealand equipped to permit him his resolute self-rescue? Did he steal his birthright by the simple act of flight, or were there other contingencies—of hardship, or independence, or both? And did he, perchance, ironically forfeit his victory through a second abruption which turned out to be less an escape than a captivity?

In the years after the New Zealand sojourn, we know Butler less and less as a personality and more and more as a mind, which is the way he no doubt deliberately intended and contrived we should. He painted (but not successfully enough to satisfy himself) and studied the history of art; wrote *Erewhon* to enjoy his only solid success; wrote (and immured in his desk) *The Way of All Flesh;* undertook single-handedly the refutation of Darwinism in a series of self-published books which kept him engaged for years reading at the British Museum; branched into Homeric and Shakespearian scholarship; wrote a sequel to *Erewhon* near the end of his life. That, in brief, is what literary history has to say of him. Outwardly, he pursued the life of a gentleman of limited means; inwardly, he battled with the Erewhonian Ydgrunites, the Musical Banks, the Colleges of Unreason, the Priests of Sunchildism. The New Zealand years—"soul-saving" years—thrust into his life a watershed between a young manhood of frustration and cross-purposes and a later career of other frustrations and cross-purposes in addition to what many might deem eccentricity, but at least an eccentricity self-motivated and self-sustained.

Why he chose New Zealand instead of Australia will become ap-

8

parent later, but we may remind ourselves here that either of these two places seemed at the moment more desirable than most other opportunities for emigration. Experience had more than proved out the possibilities in Australia, and although New Zealand had as yet no gold (she was to have this, too, in a very short while), by all the voluminous accounts available this newest "Southern Britain" was an even likelier spot for the sons of gentlemen-clergymen, several of whom had already emigrated.

The English have more than enough spirit of adventure in them to relish Butler's preliminary chapters in the Erewhon books and all of that neglected volume, *A First Year in Canterbury Settlement,* especially the parts about mountaineering. Still, the Englishman prefers to go out from "Home" and at length to come back, even as Butler did. Though he may have only small expectations of returning, he will maintain the fiction; his pioneering is predicated on the idea of return. He will tend to think of himself, consequently, as a human constant among natural variables, whereas other kinds of pioneers—Americans, for instance, or more accurately the European migrants who became Americans—may show themselves more adaptable to circumstances.

Butler could point to family precedent for wanderlust in the person of a great-great-uncle James, who "after some scrape" went out (in 1764) to serve the East India Company at about the same time Captain Cook was rediscovering New Zealand. Uncle James had been a surgeon, artist, and engineer; Butler liked him especially for his interest in art, and for his having got into a scrape. A hundred years later, the great-grandnephew was to embark for not altogether different reasons. And the same great-grandnephew who in his *Life of Dr. Samuel Butler* (Samuel's grandfather) admired Uncle James's letters home was fated to have his own letters published, not by posterity but by parent, as *A First Year in Canterbury Settlement* (1863). He was most unhappy with the result, he always said, but to others the book gave just enough about his life in New Zealand to make them want to know more.

Views about Butler's New Zealand residence have been less extensive than various. They range all the way from Muggeridge's curt

9

verdict (in *The Earnest Atheist*) of "no adventure" because "roughing
it did not really appeal to him,"[2] to Fort's assertion (*Samuel Butler*)
that in New Zealand (where everything was "simple, rough, and
wholesome"), free from all the complications and agitations of civilized life, Butler matured and was invigorated. The full evidence does
not suit with either extreme, but the facts tend in Fort's direction. *The
Way of All Flesh* deals only with the preliminaries to emigration.*

Butler's New Zealand venture, then, was far from unique—very
little more headstrong, perhaps, than the behavior of any normal youth
of ability and integrity who does not quite see eye to eye with his
parents. But in this instance it was undertaken only after lengthy and
apparently rather acrimonious negotiations between father and son.
(On this point we have chiefly the son's testimony.) Canon Butler,
favoring law or teaching as a compromise alternative to the church,
was dubious whether Sam could succeed as a farmer; but rather than
see him in the "very dangerous society" of London artists he finally
consented to the proposal for emigration. Having granted this much,
and having abruptly dismissed a scheme for cotton-growing in Liberia,
he still argued that South Africa or "even Columbia" (probably the
Pacific Northwest) would be nearer than New Zealand. At last, however, New Zealand it was to be—partly, no doubt, because of the
religious background of the Canterbury settlement.

That a lingering taint still hung over the idea of emigration is evident from these negotiations in themselves, and it was perceptible not

---

* Although the novel reveals Ernest Pontifex as toying with the idea of
emigration through several chapters, during and immediately following the
term in prison, it does not finally take him into exile. First, Ernest resolves to
"take what remained of his money, go off to America or Australia and never
be heard of more"; then he thinks specifically of gold fields in either country,
where he might make a fortune; next it is either Australia or New Zealand.
Theobald offers to pay his passage, but he meets and marries Ellen only to find
himself trapped, as he supposes, and again he thinks of flight: except for the
children, "he would have left her and gone to America." As it turns out, it is
Ellen herself who goes to America with "Bill the butcher's man," and with
this resolution of affairs the emigration motif is dropped. Strict literalness
would have given us some New Zealand chapters for *The Way of All Flesh,*
and interesting chapters they would have been.

only in England but in the colonies as well, as one of the letters from Charlotte Godley (wife of John Robert Godley, founder of Canterbury Settlement), written in 1851, makes clear:

> In a Colony, one comes across such curious people; it seems very un-gracious to say so, but unconsciously one becomes almost a little afraid of new-comers, unless one knows something about them. If anyone gets into a scrape, or makes a bad marriage—"Oh, go out to New Zealand (or some other very distant colony) where no one will know anything about it." One is sometimes disposed to feel a little indignant about it, but in fact, it is a very good and right thing that there should be a place where people can, as it were, begin over again; and if they will only not call very early in the morning, and not sit very long, I am sure I have no right to complain.[3]

Some of this no doubt was in the Canon's mind. But "a good and right thing" it was for the son, as things turned out, though in both hindsight and foresight it may be regarded as touch and go.* It would be up to Sam to prove to his father that after all he *could* succeed, and much in *A First Year* has the ring of self-justification. Made up as it was from Sam's letters home, arranged for the press and published by that same father who had been so dubious of the venture, the book would naturally bear such a tone. On the other hand, Canon Butler's acts of editorship and publication may be taken as not too grudging an admission that Sam was right after all. At any rate, the New Zealand arrangement fit easily enough into current patterns. Emigration was in full tide from Britain as well as from other European lands; emigration to the Canterbury Settlement, moreover, was of a highly selective char-

---

* Butler in later years said or wrote so little about his New Zealand sojourn that he might be suspected of suppressing it for some special reason, particu-larly in view of his attitude toward *A First Year*. Mrs. Godley, however, according to the testimony of her granddaughter, was similarly taciturn:

Looking back, I cannot recall that she ever spoke much of her New Zealand experi-ences. They were stored in her mind; but she disliked talking of herself, and seldom did so, except for very special reasons. . . . It seemed almost impossible to associate her with that primitive life—to use their friend Mr. FitzGerald's words—"on the shores of a scarcely inhabited island."—*Letters from Early New Zealand,* pp. xviii–xix.

acter—nothing for any gentleman or gentleman's son, with or without means, to be much ashamed of.

The amount being written about New Zealand was in itself some measure of the antipodean magnetism. Butler must have read rather widely; it is hardly reasonable to suppose that a young university graduate intending to try his fortune in New Zealand would not have informed himself as thoroughly as he could on what the land had to offer. By 1859 there was more than enough reading matter at hand: "ninety volumes, two hundred pamphlets, and nearly a hundred-weight of parliamentary papers," according to Dr. Arthur S. Thomson, whose *Story of New Zealand,* published during that year, made still another. Many or most of these books were available in both England and New Zealand. They followed a fairly consistent pattern: some attention to the physical features of the country, much about Maori traits and customs, something about the opportunities for successful emigration. A few were purely descriptive, but most contained advice of one kind or another, directly expressed or strongly implied. We do not know what, specifically, Butler read—as much, very likely, as he could get his hands on. In a short time his own book would become part of this utilitarian library of colonial information.

Reading, however, could not have suggested altogether adequately the rapidity with which the new country was being taken up. What Butler did not know might well have deterred him: the fact that upon arrival, it would be necessary for him to seek a base of operations in the remotest corners of the settlement and that, furthermore, he might consider himself fortunate to find even this. But such was the circumstance which took him to Mesopotamia Station and gave us *Erewhon.*

MESOPOTAMIA

*I am there now, as I write; I fancy that I can see
the downs, the huts, the plain, and the river-bed—
that torrent pathway of desolation, with its distant
roar of waters. Oh, wonderful! wonderful! so
lonely and so solemn . . .*

EREWHON

The most picturesque and exciting time of Samuel Butler's life was
the part that he wanted least known. During the New Zealand
ays themselves, to be sure, he showed little enough of the feline in-
:inct for concealment that later became so prominent a trait in
is character. No man ever worked more diligently than the London
utler, the Butler of Clifford's Inn, at making himself into a legend. It
mused him, it seems, to produce an idealized self-portrait through a
ainstaking selection of those ideas and events by which he wished to
e remembered by posterity. In this he was abetted by Henry Festing
nes, whose two-volume memoir attempted the role of Boswell to
utler's late-Victorian Johnson. *The Way of All Flesh* did its part too,
shaping the image of the injured son, more sinned against than sin-
ing. We have, as the result of all this, a highly selective Samuel Butler
-possibly more highly selective than the man himself in his more
rthright moods might have preferred. Because he strove so mightily

13

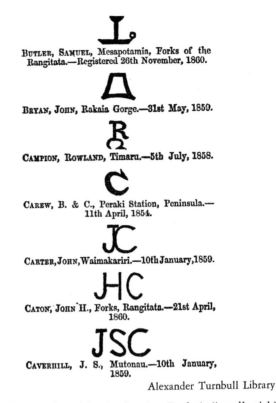

BUTLER, SAMUEL, Mesapotamia, Forks of the Rangitata.—Registered 26th November, 1860.

BRYAN, JOHN, Rakaia Gorge.—31st May, 1859.

CAMPION, ROWLAND, Timaru.—5th July, 1858.

CAREW, B. & C., Peraki Station, Peninsula.—11th April, 1854.

CARTER, JOHN, Waimakariri.—10th January, 1859.

CATON, JOHN H., Forks, Rangitata.—21st April, 1860.

CAVERHILL, J. S., Mutonau.—10th January, 1859.

Page from an old sheep-brand book, showing Butler's "candlestick" brand

to win and preserve the reputation of sage rationalist, he was impelled to suppress the romantic that was also in him. Was it compatible with a position of sage rationality that he had begun his career as a colonial? It was not; therefore he chose to let people believe that he had really not begun it thus; that the New Zealand years were a freakish interlude of no lasting significance.

Butler had been, in effect, not only a colonial but even a colonial land-speculator and woolmonger. Having revealed all this in *A First Year in Canterbury Settlement,* did he decide that remembrance of such conduct was inappropriate to the status he had finally achieved? If so, he was not the first or the last colonial gone "Home" to think this way. He must be charged with some measure of such vanity, for *A*

14

First Year, of all his books, was the one he tried deliberately to bury in oblivion. To this book, as almost to an unpublished memoir, we must turn for the un-Butlerian picture of colonial sheepman, bullock-driver, land-rusher: the squatter squire of Mesopotamia. Indeed, to the leisurely career of gentleman, the "nice person" type that he came to regard so highly, New Zealand was no proper prelude. His whole connection with the colony had been altogether precipitate; it had lacked dignity, delicacy, deliberation. Even with capital at his disposal he had to scheme and scramble for the piece of land that was to become famous for his having lived on it.

Land rushes, like gold rushes, often produce near-panic. In a way, a land rush is hardly more than an attenuated gold rush that keeps the diggers a little more widely separated: the suspense, the anxiety, the chicanery, the disappointment are all there, though they normally work themselves out in less spectacular fashion than in the gold seams. And even the best-intentioned accounts of what is taking place are dubious guides for prospective rushers, especially when the goal lies halfway around the world and fresh news goes stale in transit. From the standpoint of economics, what the books and the magazine pieces had to say about New Zealand was already out of date before it could reach the public. The man with capital, however, as *Erewhon* points out, is furnished with supplementary limbs, and can survive to thrive where the strong and eager poor man will wither and perish. Sam Butler did not come empty-handed, or quite empty-headed, but he must have realized soon after arrival that the situation was not what the home papers had made it out to be. In the nature of things it simply could not be; the momentum of settlement was too great for leisurely study, weighing of alternatives, and a carefully plotted approach. Still, insofar as it could be, it was a calculated risk that Butler took.

Getting to the colony took him from September, 1859, to January, 1860, aboard the *Roman Emperor.* Soon after arrival he began the extended task of looking around for a sheep run. In the process of doing so, and in talking with acquaintances (made quickly, as is common in

pioneering life), he came to realize how many others had already pre
ceded him. Substantially the same things had happened to the land i
Canterbury that happen in other newly opened countries; they ha
happened, moreover, against the intentions of the founders, and with
out always serving the best interests of either the community or th
land itself. The land taken first was obviously the best or else had th
advantage of being close to market: it went fast. Free (or nearly free
range developed on the periphery, with large holdings. Public lan
was soon being pressed into use as payment for public debts, and lan
policy developed into a hot political issue alongside pressures for easi
access and more rapid transportation. Landholding quickly became th
sign paramount of social prestige; speculation in land was, for som
the road to wealth.

A green and pleasant land it was, and is. Inhabited for sever
hundred years by the fierce but intelligent and tractable Maoris, Ne
Zealand had been discovered by Tasman in 1642 but remained ur
trodden by Europeans until Cook arrived in 1769. During the next fe
years Cook completed his monumental work of charting the islanc
and, to some extent, exploring them; but embroilments in Americ
and Europe conspired for decades against any systematic schemes c
settlement, and Cook's untimely death in Hawaii removed the mo
influential champion of the country's attractions. With the establisl
ment of penal settlements in Australia, however, and the gradual pen
tration of traders, whalers, and missionaries, "Maoriland" (as th
Australians came to call it) came slowly into the British purview
something more than a demijungle of cannibals.

Land-buying in New Zealand had commenced in the 1830's and l
1840 the total area claimed after one fashion or another by the *pakeh*
(non-Maori) was over fifty million acres. Some of it was "sold" l
both Maori and *pakeha* with little or no regard to either law or trutl
and indeed until the Treaty of Waitangi in 1840 there was litt
enough law to go by. This agreement, by which political sovereign
over New Zealand (with royal pre-emption rights on land) pass
formally from the Maoris to the Crown of England, put a virtu

16

"freeze" on much of the land, pending settlement of the numerous irregular claims. On the other hand, vast tracts were subsequently pre-empted and purchased by the Crown. When in 1853 separate provinces were created, the provincial governments became autonomous in the disposition of unoccupied ("waste") lands. Government land was made available in large holdings, and, in consequence, as D. O. W. Hall has pointed out,

> Sheepfarming was the one calling that the new-comer might hope to follow without losing his entire capital in exchange for his experience. The majority, therefore, engaged in running sheep on the empty spaces of the inland region, leasing from five to 50,000 acres at a cheap rental.[1]

Freehold was prohibitively high for most prospective landholders; besides, with reasonably satisfactory waste lands available at low rental, outright purchase was not a profitable or necessary investment: spare funds could best be put into stocking and improving the rented land.

Butler, by reason of errors in judgment not altogether of his own making, did not retain his land or leave his money in New Zealand long enough to yield much interest from the agrarian economy. Had he done so, his troubles would have been fewer and his career, it may be, more productive; but he called his money home, reinvested it (with the advice of London bankers) in a Canadian concern which, failing, swept away most of his capital.

Erewhon Revisited, almost as if to compensate imaginatively for such lack of foresight, provides that the gold which is to be bootlegged into Erewhon for George shall be invested in land, which had turned out to be the one and only financial *coup* of the author's life.

The Canterbury Settlement, in blueprint, had been envisaged as a society of modest freeholders on farms, expanding in a slow, orderly way from the periphery of a town (or towns) into the surrounding countryside—a small-scale Utopia or Erewhon with no more eccentricities than any comparable settlement of Englishmen would exhibit. This scheme was projected during the 1840's, a time that produced such other co-operative enterprises as Brook Farm and Fruitlands in

America. The organization, supported energetically by the Church of England, expected its member emigrants to invest sizable amounts of capital in acreage to which—with funds thus provided—roads might be built and in time other benefits secured: bridges, harbor facilities, places of assembly and—later—railroads, public parks, libraries, museums, and all the rest of both the necessities and luxuries it would take to reconstitute a "brighter Britain" as a present haven and an ultimate new nation. New Zealand might prove England's phoenix: the utopian note was fairly strong, strong enough to interest a good many intellectuals.

Thus the "Canterbury Pilgrims," arriving in four ships late in 1850, had no intention, originally, of developing into a squatterarchy. (The Australasian "squatter," unlike the American, was a large landholder with political influence commonly proportionate to the size of his holdings.) Having an option from the earlier New Zealand Company (now defunct) on the Canterbury Block, comprising Banks Peninsula and the plains region between the Waipara and Ashburton rivers, they intended that there should be large freehold estates for the wealthy and small freehold farms for yeomen: "The whole spirit of the Association was against cheap land and the squatting system,"[2] says L. G. D. Acland, the local historian of the Canterbury runs. But the land sold very slowly, and there was immediate pressure for money to undertake improvements. In Australia, on the other hand—a region of at least some few years' experience—squatting had been the rule. A drought there in 1850 sent a number of Australian squatters to New Zealand, and they encouraged the government to relax its regulations. (They were known as "Prophets" or "Shagroons"—"prophets" because they prophesied the failure of farming in contrast with stock-raising—and they are said in return to have nicknamed the Association's settlers the "Canterbury Pilgrims.") Partly to accommodate the Australians, in order not to lose the capital they had brought into the colony, it was decided to open the "waste" lands in "Class III" runs of 5 to 50,000 acres. In the resultant land-scramble most of the country had been pre-empted by the end of 1855, and Samuel Butler, arriving five years later, was to find himself almost too late.

Energetic effort, however, might still bring a man success. For example, the very existence of the "Mackenzie Country," southwest of Mesopotamia, had not been revealed until 1855. Even then the revelation came only after the capture of James Mackenzie, a systematic sheep-thief who used an uncommonly well-trained dog to drive the stolen sheep by night into an extensive pastoral region that only he knew about—an Erewhonian sort of land-pocket beyond Burke's Pass. Mackenzie left New Zealand shortly thereafter, under very much of a cloud, but the region he discovered still bears his name and he has become a local legend. His career furnished evidence that unknown patches of grazing land, up to the 1860's, were still theoretically discoverable.

One of the histories of Christchurch reports that bumblebees, introduced into Canterbury in the 1880's to assist the propagation of red clover, spread over the region with astonishing rapidity; letters to the newspapers recorded the appearance of the bees in distant parts almost immediately. Thirty years previously, early land-seekers had been the human insects swarming over the land; Butler was one of the last bumblebees to fly the original free-for-all pattern. It so happened that he buzzed the loudest.

To claim a run, a man merely applied at the Land Office for "a likely place of country which he had seen on his travels, often in loosely-defined terms so far as precise boundaries were concerned."[3] He bound himself to stock the run within six months with one sheep to each 20 acres or one head of cattle to every 120 acres, and had only a cheap rent to pay. This kind of high-country run, far out on the unpopulated periphery of the settlement, is clearly recognizable as the base from which the narrator of *Erewhon* takes off.

Theoretically, sheep farming was an uncomplicated procedure. The squatter

. . . put his sheep on the run and tried to keep them there. He marked the lambs when necessary and shore the sheep once a year. Until scab broke out there was no dipping, and few people had the facilities for washing sheep before shearing. Everyone tried to breed up his flock as fast as he could. Until about 1868 when all the runs were fully stocked there was always a good market for store sheep.[4]

Australian sheep had already begun coming in to certain runs held by the "Pre-Adamite" settlers (those few in Canterbury before the Pilgrims). The scrub and grassy overgrowth, when dry, burned easily. Even explorers lighted fires to burn off the scrub, and the squatters made burning a regular practice. There were no predators, and few natural enemies other than occasionally unseasonable winter blizzards, but the "scab"—an insect parasite—soon made its unwelcome appearance. Scab came in about 1854 and was particularly bad on the plains, where wire fences were introduced after 1860. Gradually, the plains stations were broken up into smaller freehold estates or still smaller farms; but except for some shrinkage, the high-country stations have not changed fundamentally to the present day.

Remarking that runholding in Canterbury has always been more or less touch-and-go economically, Acland goes on to say that

hardly one of the early squatters (except the "Shagroons") had any sheep-farming experience whatever. A few were natural sheep men who soon learnt their business, but the only thing that saved any of the others was that competent Scotch managers and shepherds were more plentiful in the old days than they have ever been since.[5]

Squatter politics—in which Butler was necessarily interested—centered of course in questions of land tenure. Not having more than a small fraction of their runs in freehold (the homestead lot itself, as a general rule), the big squatters feared that pre-emption for freehold on the part of smaller farmers would break up their runs, as in fact it would, and they would have no compensation. Consequently, they "amended the 'Amended Regulations' " to permit themselves to buy smaller acreages, one at a time, and forestall other proceedings between purchases. This took place in early 1858, the first year of William Sefton Moorhouse's superintendency, and inspired "The Song of the Squatters," by Crosbie Ward, a politician-editor-parodist of considerable ability. A parody of "Hiawatha," the poem tells how the squatter interest won a victory by outtalking the Provincial Council. After getting their way, the squatters go home:

> Then departed all the Stockmen,
> Crafty Squatters, subtle Shepherds,
> To the Southward and the Northward,
> To the deep and wide Waitangi,
> To the changing Hurunui,
> To the gloomy Harewood Forest,
> To the icy Lake of Coleridge,
> To the Country of Mackenzie,
> To the region of the Westward;
> With their thumbs up to their noses,
> And their other fingers waving,
> Chuckling at the favours granted,
> Grieving at the little asked for,
> And they kicked the farmer backward
> From the fertile spots of country
> In the region of the Westward,—
> Never thinking of hereafter.[6]

The townsmen and small landholders were naturally on the other side of the question, but at the moment the squatters held the ascendancy, as they did also in Australia.

In making his bumblebee flights into the high country, Butler explored pretty thoroughly the possibilities on the eastern slopes of the Southern Alps and even penetrated beyond the divide (at Whitcombe Pass, his own discovery). He located finally in the upper valley of the Rangitata, having actually very little choice in the matter.* But his

* "It is not generally known that Butler and his friend, John Brabazon, bought the first freehold land on the Waitangi run, which at that time also took in part of the present Te Akatarawa. In March 1863 they went south to

21

settlement at Mesopotamia by no means ended his wanderings in search of other possibilities; rather, it furnished him a convenient advance base for further operations, none of which, however, was to prove successful to the extent of providing him another run.

Settlement had quickly worked its way up the valley of the Rangitata; Peel Forest Station was under way in 1854, and Mt. Peel Station was started in 1856. The proprietors of the latter

. . . were the first farmers enterprising enough to risk stock on the higher hills. By 1855 the plains and low hills were occupied, and the partners preferred making the experiment of taking up country then supposed to be fit only for wild pigs, to expending the greater part of their capital (which was only £2000 apiece) in buying the lease of a run.[7]

A neighboring squatter, says a letter by one of the Mt. Peel proprietors, "laughed at our exploring, and said that the banks of Rangitata were perpendicular; he would not attempt to take a horse down for fifty pounds, and the opposite country impassable." To this the partners replied that "this was very likely, but we had a fancy for looking at it. (In the Colonies you always like to see for yourself, and the worse account you hear of unoccupied country, the greater the reason for going to look at it.)"[8] The Maoris (who had the reputation of a congenital inability to tell the truth) were not, it would appear, the only liars. In such men as the Mt. Peel proprietors we see the counterpart of Butler's "cadet" in *Erewhon*, who also has the urge to "see for himself"—a very common and natural desire for the time and place.

Butler's game acceptance of the life at Mesopotamia and his elation at the success he was enjoying are clearly evident throughout *A First Year in Canterbury Settlement*. Later there will be time for speculation

see Lake Wanaka, travelling on horseback and spending a night with the Teschemakers at Haldon. Brabazon was friendly with Edmund Gibson, the original owner of Waitangi, and on 30 November 1863 he and Butler bought a twenty-acre section on Tent Creek, on Gibson's property, and sold it back to him. Gibson afterwards bought several freehold sections round his homestead on Tent Creek."—Oliver A. Gillespie, *South Canterbury: A Record of Settlement* (Timaru, N.Z., South Canterbury Centennial History Committee, 1958), p. 325 n.

on the reasons why Butler denied—or tried to deny—this book a place among his writings. Here it is enough to recall that it was of Butler's authorship and his father's editorship: extracting Sam's letters home, Canon Butler put together a running account of his son's venture during the early stages and arranged to have it published—not without the precaution of first sending the manuscript to New Zealand for further editing and Sam's imprimatur. On the return journey it underwent shipwreck; so thoroughly were the mailbags soaked before being retrieved that the manuscript seemed hopelessly illegible until someone discovered that it could be read with the aid of a mirror. The book was published in July, 1863. As a book of letter reports it is characteristic both of the times and of the type of settler Butler was. A few years later his erstwhile friend and neighbor Lady Barker (wife of Frederick Napier Broome, of "Broomielaw" sheep station) published a volume called *Station Life in New Zealand* (1870), and there were other similar books. The Canterbury Pilgrims left rather a complete record, self-conscious pioneers that they were.

The "cadet" already referred to (New Zealand preferred the more dignified word to the Australian "jackeroo") is a familiar figure at most early sheep stations. Butler had two cadets with him, but only for a short time, deciding that the arrangement whereby a young man works for his board and lodging but no pay, merely "to see a little of up-country life" and learn something of stock raising, was not economically sound. However, such possibilities, as suggested in *Erewhon* itself (in the earlier days of settlement), or the longer process of working up to ownership, were open to young men. Many succeeded; they began by laboring humbly as "lizards" (musterers or apprentice shepherds) and in time were able to set themselves up on small runs on their own as "moleskin squatters," that is, gentlemen-farmers in overalls.

Since the Rangitata River figures in *Erewhon* as well as in *A First Year* and the short piece called "Crossing the Rangitata," it may be well to approach it here. All the South Island mountain streams, dangerous and unpredictable, were to be governed by one prudential rule: when they were up, one did not cross them. Butler observes that they are to be treated with respect:

On their first few experiences of one of these New Zealand rivers, people dislike them extremely; they then become very callous to them, and are as unreasonably foolhardy as they were before timorous; then they generally get an escape from drowning or two, or else they get drowned in earnest. After one or two escapes their original respect for the rivers returns, and for ever after they learn not to play any unnecessary tricks with them. Not a year passes but what each of them sends one or more to his grave; yet as long as they are at their ordinary level, and crossed with due care, there is no real danger in them whatever.[9]

North Island rivers are deep and slow enough to have afforded inland navigation to early settlers much after the fashion of certain rivers on the eastern coast of the United States: during the Maori wars, small steamers came far up the Waikato below Auckland to support the British campaign. But the southern streams, fed from glaciers and mountain cloudbursts, rush out of the high country and split themselves into innumerable smaller channels on the Canterbury Plain of mideastern South Island which in reality is their composite delta. Formidable as they are, however, they offer a certain pioneering advantage:

A river such as the Cam or Ouse would be far more difficult to cross without bridges than the Rakaia or Rangitata, notwithstanding their volume and rapidity; the former are deep in mud, and rarely have convenient places at which to get in or out; while the latter abound in them, and have a stony bed on which the wheels of your dray make no impression.[10]

Butler tells how to look for a ford "just above a spit where the river forks into two or more branches": a bar or shingle (i.e., rough alluvial stones) with shallow water generally occurs immediately above a dangerous rapid in such instances. "A very little practice and knowledge of each river," he explains, "will enable a man to detect a ford at a glance"; and it is immediately evident why such knowledge would have been indispensable. All this, to the twentieth-century air-borne observer, becomes abundantly clear, and there are still times when he has use for such information on the ground.

Leaving Christchurch on horseback, Butler had ample opportunity to contemplate the scenery—after temporary annoyance from urchins who, as he remarks in a letter, upon seeing a squatter riding out of town on the way to his sheep station, would run alongside the road crying "Baa-a-a-a-a-a!" In part, the landscape reminded him of Europe:

On the whole, if the road leading from Heathcote Ferry to Christchurch were through an avenue of trees, and the fields on either side were cultivated with Indian corn and vineyards, and if through these you could catch an occasional glimpse of a distant cathedral of pure white marble, you might well imagine yourself nearing Milan. As it is, the country is a sort of a cross between the plains of Lombardy and the fens of North Cambridgeshire.[11]

But the "ifs" were big ones, and the reality was otherwise. In the early 1860's the road out of Christchurch was "metaled" with crushed stone for some four or five miles, with fences and fields on both sides, the fences being chiefly "low ditch and bank planted with gorse, rarely with quick [hedge], the scarcity of which detracts from the resemblance to English scenery which would otherwise prevail."[12] The colonists were doing their best at reproducing "Home," even to the extent of importing the gorse which since has proliferated itself into something just short of a national calamity, but Butler found the copy "slatternly compared with the original": scarcity of both materials (especially timber) and labor bred makeshift arrangements. Even the breaks in government roads were sometimes repaired with the aid of whatever vegetation could be procured at the roadside to stop mudholes—"bad, but to a certain extent necessary, where there is so much to be done and so few hands and so little money with which to do it."[13]

Past the area of settlement lay a long stretch of the Canterbury Plain, backed by the mountains. Butler found the journey monotonous, commenting that "old Handel" would find "the 'pleasure of the plains' not very exciting in these mountains."[14]

Along the way, exploring hither and yon for land or merely on pleasure rides, Butler almost invariably encountered warm hospitality from those who had already settled. For example:

> After proceeding some few miles further I came to a station, where, though a perfect stranger, and at first (at some little distance) mistaken for a Maori, I was most kindly treated, and spent a very agreeable evening. The people here are very hospitable; and I have perceived kindness already upon several occasions, from persons upon whom I had no sort of claim.[15]

The situation of such people impressed him as more than a little desirable, perhaps enviable, though what he has to say sounds less like Samuel Butler than some colonizing agent, and needs to be read as having been produced for "Home" consumption:

> In a year or two you will find yourself very comfortable. You will get a little fruit from your garden in summer, and will have a prospect of much more. You will have cows, and plenty of butter and milk and eggs; you will have pigs, and, if you choose it, bees, plenty of vegetables, and in fact may live upon the fat of the land with very little trouble, almost as little expense. If you grudge this, your fare will be rather unvaried, and will consist solely of tea, mutton, bread, and possibly potatoes. For the first year, these are all you must expect; the second will improve matters; and the third should see you surrounded with luxuries.[16]

However, he was almost certainly sincere in saying this and very likely in believing, at the time, that he could be won over to the simplicity of the pioneering way of life. His critique of that way is interesting:

New Zealand seems far better adapted to develop and maintain in health the physical than the intellectual nature. The fact is, people here are busy making money; that is the inducement which led them to come in the first instance, and they show their sense by devoting their energies to the work. Yet, after all, it may be questioned whether the intellect is not as well

26

schooled here as at home, though in a very different manner. Men are as shrewd and sensible, as alive to the humorous, and as hardheaded. Moreover, there is much nonsense in the old country from which people here are free. There is little sectarianism, and, as a general rule, a healthy, sensible tone of conversation, which I like very much. But it does not do to speak about John Sebastian Bach's Fugues or pre-Raphaelite pictures.[17]

At length Butler found a provisional end to his wanderings in a bit of "country" worth a try. Farther up the Rangitata than what is now the hamlet of Peel Forest (a summer camping resort) is Forest Stream: "an ugly, barren-looking place enough," Butler said of it, ". . . a deep valley between two high ranges, which are not entirely clear of snow for more than three or four months in the year. As its name implies, it has some wood, though not much, for the Rangitata back country is very bare of timber."[18] It was up Forest Stream several miles that Butler first set up a temporary homestead in a V-hut. He had purchased 20 acres of freehold as a site (still held in his name, it was discovered a few years ago in a survey of delinquent tax-rolls) and spent the first winter there testing out the possibilities of wintering sheep. Concerning the right location of a homestead he has special advice:

The first question is, Where shall you place your homestead? You must put it in such a situation as will be most convenient for working the sheep. These are the real masters of the place—the run is theirs, not yours: you cannot bear this in mind too diligently. All considerations of pleasantness of site must succumb to this. You must fix on such a situation as not to cut up the run, by splitting off a little corner too small to give the sheep free scope and room. They will fight rather shy of your homestead, you may be certain; so the homestead must be out of their way. You *must,* however, have water and firewood at hand, which is a great convenience, to say nothing of the saving of labour and expense. Therefore, if you can find a bush near a stream, make your homestead on the lea side of it. A stream is a boundary, and your hut, if built in such a position, will interfere with your sheep as little as possible.[19]

By June, 1860, he had completed and was occupying his V-hut:

27

June 1860.—The V-hut is a *fait accompli,* if so small an undertaking can be spoken of in so dignified a manner. It consists of a small roof set upon the ground; it is a hut, all roof and no walls. I was very clumsy, and so, in good truth was my man. Still, at last, by dint of perseverance, we have made it wind and water tight. It was a job that should have taken us about a couple of days to have done in first-rate style; as it was, I am not going to tell you how long it *did* take.[20]

We need to remember that June means winter in New Zealand, and that winter in the Canterbury high country brings snow and ice. After this first season of roughing it in the hut, Butler concluded that he could not winter sheep in the restricted area near Forest Stream; he therefore bought leasehold at Mesopotamia and abandoned the V-hut, but not without paying it a tribute in farewell:

I did so with some regret, for we had good fare enough in it, and I rather liked it; we had only stones for seats, but we made splendid fires, and got fresh and clean snow-grass to lie on, and dried the floor with wood ashes. Then we confined the snow-grass within certain limits by means of a couple of poles laid upon the ground and fixed into their places with pegs; then we put up several slings to hang our saddle-bags, tea, sugar, salt, and bundles, etc.; then we made a horse for the saddles—four riding saddles and a packsaddle—and underneath this went our tools at one end and our culinary utensils, limited but very effective, at the other. Having made it neat we kept it so, and of a night it wore an aspect of comfort quite domestic, even to the cat, which would come in through a hole left in the thatched door for her especial benefit, and purr a regular hurricane.[21]

At times, it would appear, roughing it was not so distasteful to Butler as Muggeridge, in *The Earnest Atheist,* suggests. On one occasion, however, the bubble of domestic felicity was abruptly punctured. Having left his V-hut warm and comfortable, Butler came back days later to find the interior a quagmire: "I fear we had not put enough thatch upon it, and the ten days' rain had proved too much for it." (Local tradition reported that Butler and his man had put the bundles of thatch on upside down, but it seems more likely that they had simply failed to provide a roof sufficiently heavy to turn a protracted downpour of mountain rain.) The homecoming was a soggy affair:

It was now neither air-tight nor water-tight; the floor or rather the ground, was soaked and soppy with mud; the nice warm snow-grass, on which I had lain so comfortably the night before I left, was muddy and wet; altogether there being no fire inside, the place was as revolting-looking an affair as one would wish to see: coming wet and cold off a journey, we had hoped for better things. There was nothing for it but to make the best of it, so we had tea, and fried some of the beef—the smell of which was anything but agreeable, for it had been lying ten days on the ground on the other side the Rangitata, and was, to say the least, somewhat high—and then we sat in our great-coats on four stones around the fire, and smoked; then I baked, and one of the cadets washed up; and then we arranged our blankets as best we could, and were soon asleep, alike unconscious of the dripping rain, which came through the roof of the hut, and of the cold raw atmosphere, which was insinuating itself through the numerous crevices of the thatch.[22]

Later (February 6, 1863), after Butler had moved to the present location of Mesopotamia homestead, a similar thing happened. Edward Chudleigh, a Peel Forest Station cadet who had taken employment at Mesopotamia at the time, records in his diary: "The hurricane . . . blew great guns and took a deal of thatch off our house. Butler could look from his bed through the roof, a large peice [*sic*] being taken clean off."[23] Chudleigh, who mentions Butler at several other places in his diary, was likewise a clergyman's son, and felt the urge to explore just as did the young cadet in *Erewhon*.

Did Butler in fact actually build the house he lived in? There is some doubt, in view of the circumstances of the famous horse race to Christchurch with J. H. Caton, who had taken over a neighboring run and built his hut on Butler's lease-land. "In those days," says Acland, "next to sheep-stealing or introducing scab, the most unneighborly thing a squatter could do was buy freehold on his neighbour's run."[24] And that is what Caton—to keep possession of his hut and site—was determined to do. The hundred-mile dash to the Land Office, as re-

A race to the Land Office

L. J. Kennaway, *Crusts*

counted in *A First Year,* is one of the more exciting episodes of Butler's New Zealand career.

When Butler took up the Mesopotamia run, a government survey
revealed that Caton had already erected a shepherd's hut well within
Butler's boundaries. Since this was on the most desirable site for his
own purposes, Butler tried first of all to arbitrate with Caton and let a
third party fix compensation for the loss of the hut. Caton would not
agree to this. The alternative, as both men well understood, would be
for one of them to buy the tract as freehold, for neither, under leasehold, actually owned it. Each also understood that the other would
undoubtedly proceed to the Land Office in Christchurch and try to
make the purchase, at £2 per acre: a small investment, comparatively
speaking, for a considerable advantage.

Butler started to Christchurch on horseback on the afternoon of the
same day he had failed to negotiate with Caton. He "camped down"
after crossing and recrossing the Ashburton River several times. Early
next morning Caton caught up with him and they rode for a time together, "each of us, of course, well aware of the other's intentions, but
too politic to squabble about them when squabbling was no manner of
use."[25] This was on a Wednesday morning; and the land board, nearly
a hundred miles distant, was to meet at ten, on Thursday. The matter
boiled down to who should reach the Land Office first and file applica-

tion for the land. With sixty miles still to go, Butler's horse gave out, but he was able to get a fresh one at one of the stations on the way. Twenty-five miles out, in the predawn darkness, he passed an accommodation house and learned that Caton was staying there. He pressed on, but was caught in a heavy rain and was forced to put up some twelve miles from town. Arriving in Christchurch early in the morning, he waited until 9:40 to go to the Land Office, and, if Caton was there, to have it out with him. The rest of the story is in Butler's words, with his substitution of "G——" for the name of Caton:

If it came to fists I should get the worst of it—that was a moral certainty—and I really half-feared something of the kind. To my surprise, the office doors were open—all the rooms were open—and on reaching that in which the application book was kept, I found it already upon the table. I opened it with trembling fingers, and saw my adversary's name written in bold handwriting, defying me, as it were, to do my worst.

The clock, as the clerk was ready to witness, was twenty minutes before ten. I learnt from him also that G—— had written his name down about half an hour [ago]. This was all right. My course was to wait till after ten, write my name, and oppose G——'s application as having been entered unduly, and before land office hours. I have no doubt that I should have succeeded in gaining my point in this way, but a much easier victory was in store for me.

Running my eye through the list of names, to my great surprise I saw my own among them. It had been entered by my solicitor, on another matter of business, the previous day, but it stood next *below* G——'s. G——'s name, then, had clearly been inserted unfairly, out of due order. The whole thing was made clear to the Commissioners of the Waste Lands, and I need not say that I effected my purchase without difficulty. A few weeks afterwards, allowing him for his hut and yard, I bought G—— out entirely.[26]

From this testimony it seems likely that whatever residence Butler finally provided for himself had been at least begun by Caton.

Whoever it was that built—or, it may be, completed or supplemented—the Mesopotamia hut, he was obliged to use whatever he found handy to the purpose. "Squatters soon learn to be their own architects," says Robert B. Booth, who saw the back-country houses through eyes already turned toward engineering design, "and very good ones many of them turned out."[27] In functionalist theory, the squatter-architects made a virtue of necessity; form followed function, and inescapably the buildings "organically" reflected the character of the surroundings. This was truer in the back blocks and the high country than elsewhere, but even there not altogether true, for in a short while Victorian ornamentation was being resolutely lugged in by bullock dray. The earliest structures, however, were nothing if not plain and honest; all the surviving photographs and sketches of the Mesopotamia huts show them to have been strictly in the raw-boned tradition.

Sheep farming was an opportunity to invest capital and learn a business without an unduly serious risk of ruin. And Butler, as a "new chum," had to "eat his toot"*—that is, get his feet on the ground and become a New Zealander. A man was designated "new chum," one account has it, until after he had passed certain ordeals; he had to "be able to ride a buckjumper, or at any rate, hold on till the saddle went, use a stockwhip, cut up and light a pipe of tobacco with a single wax vesta while riding full speed in the teeth of a sou-wester, and be ready and competent to take a hand at any manual labour going."[28] The last, probably, was the only really binding requirement in the lot, but Butler would have been game for most of them. He really wanted to learn; to belong. We see him learning when, sleeping on the ground under the stars, he discovers the trick of finding a hollow for his hipbone. Horsemanship was another lesson. "You know how bad a horseman I am," he wrote to his relatives; but this deficiency was soon made up.

There were psychological adjustments as well. In late March, 1860, in the high country, he saw a sheep killed—his first encounter with

---

* "Toot" (*tutu*) is a shrub poisonous to sheep and cattle when eaten on an empty stomach; stock affected by the plant are said to be "tooted." "The only chance for them," says R. B. Booth, "is to bleed them by driving in the blade of a small knife each side of the nose. The blood will flow black and thick, and the animal will speedily recover, but delay is fatal."—*Five Years in New Zealand*, p. 33.

butchery: "It is rather unpleasant, but I suppose I shall get as indifferent to it as other people are by and by. To show you that knives of the establishment are numbered, I may mention that the same knife killed the sheep and carved the mutton we had for dinner."[29] The cooking required his attention, along with the dishwashing; "[Take your] full part in the culinary process," he advises, "or you will soon find dissatisfaction in the camp." Cooks were hard to come by; still,

It is a great nuisance to come in from a long round after sheep and find the fire out and no hot water to make tea, and to have to set to work immediately to get your men's supper; for they cannot earn their supper and cook it at the same time. The difficulty is that good boys are hard to get, and a man that is worth anything at all will hardly take to cooking as a profession. Hence it comes to pass that the cooks are generally indolent and dirty fellows, who don't like hard work.[30]

How many would there be to cook for? At least a "couple of good bush hands," a bullock driver, and a shepherd—say, five or six in all including the squatter or (later, fortune permitting) his manager. If one ran more than two or three thousand sheep another shepherd would be necessary; and of course at shearing there would be musterers and shearers to feed. An oft-quoted passage from the *Note-Books* describes Butler's ritual of washing dishes—doing the knives first since "it might please God to take me before I came to the forks." The Mesopotamian diet, at first, was undoubtedly much the same as Butler ate at a country home soon after his arrival—"cold boiled mutton and bread, and cold tea without milk"—and with hot mutton and hot tea occasionally for variety. For the most part they lived on meat, either beef or mutton. An anecdote from the reminiscences of Albert Gray, who lived at Blackford (one of the hill stations between the Rakaia and the Rangitata) in the 1860's, is revealing:

On one of my journeys from the Rakaia Gorge I met near Horarata John Studholme, recently married. He asked me to lunch. Roast lamb was offered me. I had never before seen roast lamb eaten in New Zealand. I suppose my astonishment was written on my face. Studholme was apologetic and explained that his wife liked to have roast lamb occasionally. I could see that his conscience was uneasy about it, and well it might be. To eat a lamb which at that time without further expense would grow into a sheep and moreover give one or two fleeces of valuable wool, was to flout all correct ideas of economy. This came of matrimony. I cannot positively assert that lamb had never before been eaten in Canterbury (there was one other recently married squatter), but I can say that I had never seen it eaten, nor ever heard of such a thing.[31]

On one of the Canterbury runs, it was reported, five men ate a hundred pounds of meat a week when there were no potatoes or other vegetables; when these came, the meat consumption went down to about sixty pounds a week. Mesopotamia no doubt was little different; it was virtually impossible to vary the diet.

Taking care of the sheep was not a toilsome, full-time occupation for everyone on the run, but it was exacting in the same way it always has been since Biblical times: "You must remember they are your masters, and not you theirs; you exist for them, not they for you."[32] Since the sheep would not travel more than ten miles a day, driving them to the run was in itself a tedious business, particularly with rivers to be crossed. This process, as Butler describes it for a "small mob" of seven or eight hundred, driven by three men and two dogs, involves first of all the selection of a proper crossing: a good shelving entry and landing place with the current set toward the opposite bank, and no *tutu* nearby. Next, you "dog them, bark at them yourself furiously, beat them, spread out arms and legs to prevent their escaping, and raise all the unpleasant din about their ears that you possibly can." After they have entered the water, a man gets into the river below them and splashes water at them to keep them from getting lower in the stream than they should. The crossing described here was made during a nor'wester blowing sand in the eyes and followed by torrential rain bringing a "fresh" and threatening to maroon the drivers on a river island. However, says Butler, philosophically: "In a life of continual excitement one thinks very little of these things. They may, however, serve to give English readers a glimpse of some of the numerous incidents which, constantly occurring in one shape or other, render the life of a colonist not only endurable, but actually pleasant."[33]

But if sheep driving could be "actually pleasant"—by reason of the comparatively tractable nature of sheep, or some other circumstance—the same could scarcely be said for bullock driving. William Rolleston (of Emmanuel College, Cambridge, 1855), proprietor of Mt. Algidus Station and a friend of Butler's, had the reputation of being the best bullock driver in Canterbury and was forever proud of it. Afterward superintendent of the Province and prominent in national politics, Rolleston, says Acland,

. . . was said to be prouder of being the best bullock driver in Canterbury than anything else. As a matter of fact, he told me once that his reputation was greater than he deserved. He said he was not in a class by himself as a bullock driver, but just a "very good bullock driver indeed!"[34]

It was local folklore that instead of swearing at his bullocks, Rolleston addressed them in Greek or Latin.* Be this as it may, he and other local classicists filled the surrounding country (near Lake Coleridge) with names such as Acheron, Scamander, Simois.

Bullock driving was necessary both going to and coming from a station unless a special trip was made alone on horseback. A day's haul of supplies en route to the station, or of wool-packs from it, was fif-

---

* Although Rolleston's classical conversation with his bullocks has occasionally been attributed to Butler, we are probably justified in assuming that Butler addressed his wandering team in primitive Anglo-Saxon. As the traveling comedian Thatcher sang,

> If nice expressions you would learn,
> Colonial and new,
> Some bullock driver who is bogged
> Is just the man for you.

And an early New Zealand parson is reported to have said, in an outpouring of brotherly love, "Even a bullock driver has a soul to be saved" (S. J. Baker, *New Zealand Slang,* p. 47). Butler's bullock driver had not only a soul but a Mass book, from which was read the burial service for Dr. Andrew Sinclair, a botanist drowned in the Rangitata near Mesopotamia in 1861.

teen to twenty miles. Bullocks were scarce, costing between £20 and £30 apiece—half the price of a good horse. The usual team was eight, hitched in four pairs. Butler had only six, but they were good ones, "worth many a team of eight." But however effective they may have been (a good team was supposed to be able to draw two to three tons along a "pretty good road"), they *would* run off at night. During a single trip they strayed twice—once ten miles, the next time five—and

L. J. Kennaway, *Crusts*

Bringing home lost bullocks

the annoyance involved in finding them, Butler assures us, will deprive them of any claims for mercy. This is the sad situation of the bullock hunter:

Let him go straining his eyes examining every dark spot in a circumference many long miles in extent. Let him gallop a couple of miles in this direction and the other, and discover that he has only been lessening the distance between himself and a group of cabbage-trees; let him feel the word "bullock" eating itself in indelible characters into his heart, and he will refrain from mercy to working bullocks as long as he lives. But as there are few

36

positive pleasures equal in intensity to the negative one of release from pain, so it is when at last a group of six oblong objects, five dark and one white, appears in remote distance, distinct and unmistakable. Yes, they are our bullocks; a sigh of relief follows, and we drive them sharply home, gloating over their distended tongues and slobbering mouths.[35]

Such treatment is a disciplinary measure as well as a personal satisfaction:

If there is one thing a bullock hates worse than another it is being driven too fast. His heavy lumbering carcase is mated with a no less lumbering soul. He is a good, slow, steady, patient slave if you let him take his own time about it; but don't hurry him. He has played a very important part in the advancement of civilization and the development of the resources of the world, a part which the more fiery horse could not have played; let us then bear with his heavy trailing gait and uncouth movements; only next time we will keep him tight, even though he starve for it. If bullocks be invariably driven sharply back to the dray, whenever they have strayed from it, they will soon learn not to go far off, and will be cured even of the most inveterate vagrant habits.[36]

Butler, says Festing Jones, used to say that when he died the word "bullocks" would be found written on his heart. As late as 1897 he refers to bullock hunting in a letter,[37] and in *Erewhon Revisited,* he says, "he tried to project his mind into those of the Professors as though they were a team of straying bullocks whose probable action he must determine before he set out to look for them."[38]

Acland observes that "in all station diaries of the 'fifties,' there is continual mention . . . of hunting for lost stock and of neighbors coming in search of theirs," and Kennaway relates that on one occasion no less a personage than Bishop Harper showed up on foot at a back-country hut, having somehow or other lost his horse.[39] Kennaway also bears out what *A First Year*—and another spot or two in Butler—has to say about bullocks:

It's all very well to talk of being kind to animals, and keeping your temper, and not getting riled,—but I'll back a pair of wild New Zealand or Australian bullocks, against any living thing, to raise a man's fur to the extremest extent of exasperation and stiver.[40]

After several pages quite reminiscent of *A First Year,* ending with driving the bullocks home with a whip and maliciously enjoying it (see the illustration p. 36), Kennaway says "my sympathies are entirely with the squatter."[41]

But difficult as the bullock might be, Butler realized he was necessary and useful as one more servant to the sheep, "the masters." The sheep, like the hypothetical machines in *Erewhon,* converted man into a slave to minister to them. The first thing to do was to teach them their boundaries, with the help of dogs. Sometimes "boundary dogs" were chained to stakes on the boundaries to bark at the sheep and frighten them back, but the practice was considered cruel. Occasionally a station nearer civilization would be troubled by wild dogs; domestic cats too reverted, and lived off the birds. Butler took out to Mesopotamia a cat which bore a litter of kittens, and in one of the Darwinian letters to *The Press* he speaks of wild cats. For hunters there were the "Captain Cookers"—fierce, wild descendants of the English pigs Cook had turned loose in the islands nearly a century earlier. Cattle and sheep also occasionally reverted.

None of these creatures, with the possible exception of the rare wild dogs, offered any threat to the life of sheep or lamb; the only real predator was a mountain parrot, the kea, which would sometimes attack a crippled or snow-bound sheep, tearing through the wool and flesh on its back to find the fat around the kidneys. The scab, however, was another matter. This highly mobile insect parasite, once it started, could quickly infect a whole flock: "A sheep severely infected with scab becomes a pitiful object. The body gets covered with a yellow scaly substance, the wool falls off or is rubbed off in patches, the disease causing intense itchiness, the animal loses flesh and appetite, and unless relieved sickens and dies."[42] Dipping was the cure and preventive, and a scab-infested flock—under severe financial penalties for failure to comply—had to be dipped and thinned out until clean.

The scab ruined the prospects of many a squatter, especially in the lower country.

Because of its isolation by river barriers (Forest Stream and the Rangitata) Butler's station came by its name, Mesopotamia, rather naturally. Through this same isolation, it was rendered practically scab-proof; so the name had an economic as well as a poetic significance, Butler was to discover. Even so, it was perhaps a bit fanciful. The usual station name was either reminiscent of "Home" (Oakleigh, Rokeby, Malvern Hills), or taken from a local geographical feature (Blue Cliff, Mt. Fourpeaks, Mt. Peel)—in a sense "Mesopotamia" belongs in this class—or taken from the Maori. "Mesopotamia" is euphonious enough to suit with Maori appellatives like Wakanui, Pakihi, Raukapuka, Kakahu, Arowhenua, and Mimimoto (later Double Corner). Rolleston's Mt. Algidus (from the Latin *algidus,* "cold") of course suited his classical taste, and there may be significance in the fact that G. S. Sale, one of the station managers in the area and later an editor of *The Press,* ended his days as professor of classics at the University of Otago (1870–1897).[43]

Grassland was developed by the systematic and—from the naturalist's point of view—ruthless use of fire. "Fire in the fern" is (or has been) a New Zealand idiom for trouble, and in thick bush or timber country it might well be used in that sense. In Canterbury, however, most of the scrub was comparatively light, especially in the high country, and no catastrophic forest fires resulted from careless burning. At the same time, bird life was largely obliterated and many native plants became scarce. Some of these, such as wild anise, gave the early mutton a particularly gamey savor that it later lost. Now and then a hut would be caught in the path of the flames, and when a neighbor's fire got out of control it was necessary to undertake the arduous and risky effort of backfiring to protect parts of a run on which there were sheep. Sometimes fire was used to clear a short cut for driving the sheep, particularly to avoid passing through scab country. Annual burning was thus by far the easiest way of clearing the scrub and, in fact, the only practicable way of handling large areas. But it brought its penalties in the form of rockslides on the hills, and in 1868 Christchurch underwent a severe flood attributable at least in part to the denuding of the hill country, which had accelerated runoff.

Shearing, which took place in the spring (late in the calendar year) brought to the station a number of temporary hands who had to be accommodated and fed. The going wage for shearers was from £1 to £1 5*s*. per hundred sheep, customarily on a contract basis, and though a good shearer could clip a hundred or more fleeces a day, the average for a gang was nearer seventy-five. Sometimes the sheep were washed before shearing; at other times they were shorn "in the grease," greasy wool bringing a somewhat lower price. Into the woolpress went the fleeces, around a hundred of them compressing into a bale nine feet long and four feet square and weighing somewhere in the neighborhood of 350 pounds. The reader of *Erewhon* is taken briefly inside a shearing shed for the memorable first encounter with Chowbok.

Shearing past, there remained the tedious journey to the coast, calling for all the strength of the bullock team and all the persuasions of the bullock driver. If the team and driver did not "camp down" along the track, there were only the barest of accommodations, many and quite possibly most of them inns resembling one on the Rakaia some fifty miles from Christchurch described by Booth as "a weird-looking habitation, a long, low, single-storeyed desolate-looking building, partly constructed of mud and partly of green timber slabs rough from the forest." It had a small parlor, two smaller bedrooms, a bar, a kitchen, and a low shed for animals. The interior was hardly more inviting:

It was a rough place, and a rough lot of characters were not unfrequently seen there. The Jack Tar just arrived from the bush or some up-country station with a cheque for a year's wages, bent on a spree, and standing drinks all around while his money lasted, the Scottish shepherd plying liquor and grasping hands for "Auld Lang Syne," the wretched debauched crawler, the villainous-looking "lag" from "t'other side," the bullock puncher, whose every alternate word was a profane oath, the stockrider, in his guernsey shirt and knee boot with stockwhip thrown over his shoulder, engaging the attention of those who would listen with some miraculous story of his exploits, mine host smilingly dealing out the fiery poison, with now and again the presence of the dripping forder from the river, come in for his glass of grog and pipe before resuming his perilous occupation.[44]

Unless there was a fenced paddock, there was no assurance that next morning the bullocks would not be several miles away in a direction known only to themselves.

Butler, who had read in addition to *The Decline and Fall of the Roman Empire* Liebig's *Agricultural Chemistry* on shipboard, must have been fairly well grounded in the theory of sheep farming, but he was flexible enough to learn empirically also. *A First Year* is the record of a young man's successful attempts at adaptation to a new and not altogether unpleasant situation. Against the contention that roughing it did not appeal to Butler may be set his passage already quoted in which pioneering is said to be "actually pleasant." The more important point, however, is that if Butler did not particularly like discomfort, neither did anyone else in the settlement. Neither does the average pioneer anywhere, for that matter; he puts up with hardship not because he has a natural hankering for it but because he must, leaving the praise of hard-scrabble life to those who have seen it only in their imaginations. The grace with which he accepts it will depend in part upon the prospects of improvement, and to Butler these appeared bright; after a year or two, he tells his readers, a station not only will have worn down its rough spots but will have developed a degree of rural affluence and ease that is quite satisfying.

The comparatively few derogatory references to the occupation of sheep farming, therefore, must be set against a general background of well-being; and anyway it did not behoove Butler in writing home to depict himself as degenerating into barbarism. The "cultivated" Englishman may be expected (today as then) to say such things as this:

I am forgetting myself into admiring a mountain which is of no use for sheep. This is wrong. A mountain here is only beautiful if it has good grass on it. Scenery is not scenery—it is "country," *subaudita voce* "sheep."

41

If it is good for sheep, it is beautiful, magnificent, and all the rest of it; if not, it is not worth looking at. I am cultivating this tone of mind with considerable success, but you must pardon me for an occasional outbreak of the old Adam.[45]

And it is just such condescension, it might be added, that the "colonials" do not easily digest, except when they have already struck the pose themselves. After that, anything goes.

All in all, Butler's view of colonial life set forth in *A First Year* reflects a good deal of satisfaction, and a letter to his aunt, Mrs. Philip Worsley, confirms this. He speaks enthusiastically of his garden, with its green peas, asparagus, potatoes; rose trees, carnations, narcissus, daffodils, poppies, stocks, sweet williams, wallflowers, larkspur—"all in two little beds on either side of the gate"—along with some dozen or more fruit trees (pear, peach, plum, cherry), several bunches of currants, and the promise of gooseberries and strawberries in another year. (This was in September of 1861.) Inside the hut are his piano, "more books than I can read," and his Cambridge pictures. He has experienced "an immense intellectual growth" which has left him "a much happier and more liberal-minded man." Some of this at least he owes to the colony itself: "I like the squatters here as a class very much. They are fine fellows. There is a more liberal feeling here than at home." As for returning to England at all soon, "I feel that I should be very unwise to do so." On the other hand, he misses the "intellectual society of clever men" and wonders if he may not be "in great danger of getting far behind." One would conclude from this letter, as from a good deal of *A First Year*, that Mesopotamia was offering very nearly all that at the moment he could reasonably demand from life. He says so quite plainly—(and with rather more sincerity than when years later he assessed his felicity at 15 Clifford's Inn):

I am perfectly satisfied. I have plenty to eat and drink, fresh air of the purest kind, good health and spirits, nice quiet steady and industrious servants, than whom I shall never have better, nor do I wish for better—what more can a mortal desire?[46]

This is the kind of satisfaction he was able to purchase through a blending of his own strenuosity with the several thousands of paternal pounds sterling. Had he come without money he might conceivably have made his way and even become prosperous, but it would certainly have taken many more years. To realize this, we have only to compare the career of one of the Mesopotamia station-hands, Robert B. Booth, whose sojourn in New Zealand was exactly contemporaneous, to within a matter of weeks, with Butler's. Arriving in August, 1859, young Booth (a boy of sixteen) free-lanced through various occupations before leaving for Australia and India in May, 1864. First it was sheep farming, during the course of which he "learned to ride stock, shoe horses, shear sheep, plough, fence, fell and split timber, and everything else that an experienced squatter ought to be able to do, not omitting the accomplishment of smoking."[47] Already inclined toward engineering (he later became a bridge-builder), Booth soon tired of the routine of station life and was off with a survey party, which offered among other inducements the sport of wild-pig hunting. Stockriding, bush-contracting for timber, and a fruitless trek to the Otago gold diggings all came in rapid succession, and in the latter part of 1861 he found himself again in Christchurch considering an offer from Samuel Butler to take a post at Mesopotamia for £60 a year, expenses paid:

I had tried most phases of a colonial life, and had gained a great deal of experience, and knew that I could always obtain remunerative employment, and after I had enjoyed a little more rambling and freedom I could decide on some fixed line to settle down upon.[48]

This kind of thing, it is evident from numerous accounts, was for young men quite "the usual." Unprovided with capital, Butler must have done the same—except, of course, that unprovided with capital he would not have come. In Australia and New Zealand alike, thousands of young men were so busy living adventure that they found no time to write it; many of them barely recorded or only hinted at experiences that would make *Erewhon* look tame.

Mesopotamia pleased Booth; he found there "the most civilised experience I had had of up-country life since I left Highfield [his first employment]," with Butler's books and piano "round a glorious fire" offering prime inducements. But despite such comforts, a chance at more bush-contracting soon took him away, though not before he had formed fast friendships with Cook (the overseer) and Butler's partner, Brabazon, who arrived about the time Booth left to do timber-cutting on the Ashburton-Rangitata track.

Butler, Booth found, was hot-tempered: "Anything approaching to ridicule where he was concerned was a mortal insult." This was proved on an occasion when Butler and Cook arranged to meet Booth at one of the boundary streams and, not finding him waiting within sight (he was napping in the shelter of a boulder), they conducted an anxious search for his drowned body. The "corpse" awoke to watch them and "could not refrain from an immoderate fit of laughter when they arrived." This, Butler could not endure: "He turned pale with passion and rode off, and I do not think he ever entirely forgave me for not being drowned when he had undertaken so much trouble to discover my body."[49] Two separate winters Booth spent some of his time at Mesopotamia, on one occasion going out with Cook and Brabazon to look for sheep drifted under the snow and missing by the narrowest of margins severe frostbite or even death from exposure. At this particular time Butler was in Christchurch to remain "for an indefinite time"; on Booth's last visit, however, he was there. "Our evenings by the fire were very enjoyable, and many a story and song went round, or Butler would play while we smoked. . . . One evening, I recollect, he told us a very remarkable ghost story, the best authenticated, as he said, he had ever heard." Briefly, the story concerned the murder of an Australian stockman by his hutkeeper, the crime being revealed by the image of the victim which on repeated occasions would appear sitting on a rail fence and then run back into the bush. With the aid of troopers and aboriginal trackers, the rancher's body was found in a pond. After conviction and sentence, the hutkeeper—who, it turned out, was a "ticket-of-leave convict well known to the police"—confessed. "I do not recollect," says Booth, "whether Butler told us if the real object of the murder transpired."[50]

"Industrious servants" Butler acquired not without some trial and error. At the high-country stations, circumstances dictated a way of life more fundamentally democratic than in some other sections of the colony, but the colonists were after all still British, and class-cleavage to a large degree held firm. There is no doubt that the station owners nearer the lowlands had an easier and pleasanter time of it. There was at all times and places an inevitable distance between man and master, but in the high country—the real frontier—this narrowed considerably. The difference is evident in comments on the one hand by Butler and on the other by Henry Tancred (later to be Sir Henry, a government minister, and chancellor of the University of New Zealand). Tancred, who in 1858 sold his share of Malvern Hills Station to Bishop Harper, believed that "no gentleman should ever do hard work with one of his men, because either the man went slow so as not to shame his employer, or the employer knocked himself up trying to get full work out of the man."[51] Butler sums up his own view by saying first that "you and your men will have to be on rather a different footing from that on which you stood in England." Supply and demand have seen to that, with the laborer soon discovering that he is at a premium. The "really good men" will not change their demeanor other than to demand high wages, but the bad ones will "assume an air of defiance which renders their immediate dismissal a matter of necessity." The inevitable shift of status had best be recognized early and acceded to: "When you have good men . . . you must recognize the different position in which you stand toward them as compared with that which subsisted at home. The fact is, they are more your equals and more independent of you, and, this being the case, you must treat them accordingly."[52]

Booth's views on this same matter are worth noting:

It is a huge mistake to suppose that the gentleman lowers himself anywhere —and especially in the Colonies—by undertaking any kind of manual labour. I have known the sons of gentlemen of good family working as bullock-drivers, shepherds, stockdrivers, bushmen, for a yearly wage, and nobody considered the employment derogatory. On the contrary, these are the men who get on and in time become wealthy.[53]

But with all this to be said, one still must not fall into the "fatal error" of submitting to disrespect, Butler goes on to point out. An unsatisfactory workman must be discharged, difficult as it may be to secure another. But

when you have men who *do* suit you, you must, besides paying them handsomely, expect them to treat you rather as an English yeoman would speak to the squire of his parish than as an English labourer would speak to him. . . . Commend yourself to a good screw for a shepherd; if he knows the value of money he knows the value of lambs, and if he has contracted the habit of being careful with his own money he will be apt to be so with yours also.[54]

Another reason for a workman's not proving satisfactory might well be alcohol. Like his counterpart in stock-raising regions the world over, the New Zealander—or, at that time, the Briton in New Zealand—worked off his frustrations, or possibly merely sought to keep himself warm, by hard drinking. In *A First Year* we encounter briefly the type to be found "knocking down" their wages in the bush taverns:

Some good hands are very improvident, and will for the most part spend their money in drinking, a very short time after they have earned it. They will come back possibly with a *dead horse to work off*—that is, a debt at the accommodation-house—and will work hard for another year to have another drinking bout at the end of it. This is a thing fatally common here. Such men are often first-rate hands and thoroughly good fellows when away from drink; but, on the whole, saving men are perhaps the best. . . . But in justice to the improvident, it must be owned they are often admirable men save in the one point of sobriety.[55]

Nor was drinking confined to the hands; the squatters themselves were susceptible to the habit:

Idle men in this country are pretty sure to take to drinking. Whether men are rich or poor, there seems to be far greater tendency here to drink than at home; and sheep farmers, as soon as they get things pretty straight and can afford to leave off working themselves, are apt to turn drunkards, unless they have a taste for intellectual employment. They find time hang heavy on their hands, and, unknown almost to themselves, fall into the practice of drinking, till it becomes a habit. I am no teetotaller, and do not want to moralize unnecessarily; still it is impossible, after a few months' residence in the settlement, not to be struck with the facts I have written above.[56]

"Intellectual employment" Butler found for himself at his piano and in writing now and then for *The Press,* not to mention the correspondence that was worked up into *A First Year.* And in this respect he was not at all exceptional, for the Canterbury bush of this particular time could show many others of his kind. Butler's description of William Rolleston's hut might fit his own or any of numerous ones that he visited. Of Rolleston himself, "a Cambridge man who took a high second-class a year or two before my time," Butler wrote:

Every now and then he leaves his up-country avocations, and becomes a great gun at the college in Christchurch, examining the boys; he then returns to his shepherding, cooking, bullock-driving, etc., etc., as the case may be. I am informed that he, having faithfully learned the ingenuous arts, has so far mollified his morals that he is an exceedingly humane and judicious bullock-driver. . . . Under his bed I found Tennyson's *Idylls of the King.* So you will see that even in these out-of-the world places people do care a little for something besides sheep.[57]

Butler goes on to tell the story of an Oxonian shepherd farther south, in Otago:

Someone came into his hut, and, taking up a book, found it in a strange tongue, and enquired what it was. The Oxonian (who was baking at the time) answered that it was *Machiavellian discourses upon the first decade of Livy.* The wonder-stricken visitor laid down the book and took up another, which was, at any rate, written in English. This he found to be Bishop Butler's *Analogy.* Putting it down speedily as something not in his line, he

47

laid hands upon a third. This proved to be *Patrum Apostolicorum Opera,* on which he saddled his horse and went right away, leaving the Oxonian to his baking.[58]

These were just such places as his own, belonging to men with whom he could feel intellectual kinship. His efforts to keep his mind alive, in all likelihood, were not only a carry-over from his college days but a stimulus from some of his neighbors. He began making authorish notes, the sort intended for development into essays. The extent to which he did so is past finding out, but the single clue appearing in the *Note-Books* is indicative:

One of the earliest notes I made, when I began to make notes at all, I found not long ago in an old book, since destroyed, which I had in New Zealand. It was to the effect that all things are either of the nature of a piece of string or a knife. That is, they are either for bringing and keeping things together, or for sending and keeping them apart. Nevertheless each kind contains a little of its opposite and some, as the railway train and the hedge, combine many examples of both.[59]

In a passage headed "Union and separation" he reverts to this idea:

In the closest union there is still some separate existence of component parts; in the most complete separation there is still a reminiscence of union. . . .

When we love, we draw what we love closer to us; when we hate a thing, we fling it away from us. All disruption and dissolution is a mode of hating; and all that we call affinity is a mode of loving.[60]

This thesis became, in fact, the central problem of his personality: dreading separation, he still could not bring himself to trust any sort of union that he could not control with entire self-convenience. For a lifetime he was to hover unhappily between the two extremes, seeking but never finding bachelor's paradise—often asserting, to be sure, that he had most certainly done so but far from proving it either to himself or to others.

Butler's problems were in essence no different from those of his

New Zealand associates; and in many respects they were easier. Nor need isolation in the country prove the undoing of a capable man: the characters and careers of his neighbors show this plainly enough. Besides Rolleston there were numerous others who had already received distinction or were to do so in the future. All of the following sizable list of worthies were at one time or another run-holders: Alexander Lean, architect of several Christchurch buildings, including the Supreme Court, and before his death in 1893 "Steward of Government Reserves, Public Trustee, Sheriff, Commander of the Canterbury volunteers and founder and first honorary conductor of the Christchurch Orchestral Society";[61] James Edward Fitzgerald, superintendent of the Province, owner of the Christchurch *Press* and national politician;* Charles Obins Torlesse, a parson's son, surveyor and mountaineer for whom Mt. Torlesse is named; Charles Hunter Brown, civil engineer; Thomas Rowley, son of the dean-designate of Christchurch Cathedral; Samuel Bealey (Cambridge, 1851), third superintendent of the Province; Marmaduke Dixon, a naval officer who was due to command a ship but liked New Zealand so well he chose to settle there in 1851; the Rev. J. Raven (Shrewsbury School and Caius College, Cambridge), vicar of Broughton Ashley for four years before emigrating in 1851. Butler's friend "Mr. Phillips" (from whose station the elaborate directions to Mesopotamia are given in "Crossing the Rangitata") was the hospitable owner of Rockwood, in the Malvern Hills. Phillips took up Rockwood in July of 1852; there were three hundred sheep there in 1854 and four thousand in 1858 (breeding and purchase)—a fair indication of how well a man might do with enough capital for a foothold.

Phillips added Point Station (between Rockwood and the Rakaia) in 1862 and finally sold Rockwood to his former cadet in 1878. Rock-

---

* "We are very angry with Mr. Fitzgerald," wrote Charlotte Godley, "for he has, I believe, quite settled to go off in the wildest possible way and join a sort of picnic sheep station. He is always, you know, after something new, and now feels behindhand because he cannot dive into all the barbarity of a station, for the mere fun of it." (*Letters from Early New Zealand*, p. 57) Mrs. Godley sympathized most particularly with Fitzgerald's wife.

wood was spoken of as a "favourite station" located "in the very heart of picturesque and romantic landscapes" and a fine place for hunting; it was visited and described by Lady Barker at about the time Butler knew it.

The other side of the picture is presented in *Chowbokiana or Notes about the Antipodes and the Antipodeans,* by "Thomas A. Scot,"* which appeared in Bombay to counteract "nonsense" about New Zealand appearing in other books. *Chowbokiana* defends the Maori and describes the *pakeha* population as a low-grade assortment with only "a few persons from the better classes of English society." The familiar charge of "Americanisation," i.e., vulgarization, is repeated, and there is much criticism of the New Zealand government under Vogel. "Life at an out-station on the plains of Canterbury, Otago, Hawke Bay, or any of the open countries suitable for merino sheep-farming," declares the author, "is most monotonous and dreary," and he concludes his volume with this blistering paragraph:

One word more in conclusion to the young gentleman of a romantic disposition who may think of crossing the Ocean, and from the Woolshed on the plain going up the Wai-Makeriri river and over the great Range, dreaming they may there see the lovely damozells who suggested the superlative Houris of EREHWON [*sic*]—they will do nothing of the kind. After travelling in a Cobb's coach and six horses, wonderfully handled by an American Jehu, seated beside Chinamen and German Jew pedlars, having matter-of-fact telegraph poles, and wire fences always in view, as they cross the treeless brown plains smothered with dust, although they will pass the Otira Gorge, one of the most romantic passes certainly traversed by a mail coach which might well indeed serve as the gate to a Terrestrial Paradise, they will arrive at the gold-diggers' town of Hokitika on the Western Sea,—they will there find only dressed-up-bar-maids from Melbourne with little curls gummed across their foreheads, serving out poisonous decoctions

* This name is signed to the Preface; the Auckland University College Library catalogue, however, lists the book as by H. Cockburn Hood. It is a pamphlet of one hundred pages, with yellow paper covers.

to half stupified diggers. Well might CHOWBOK shudder at the recollection of the people beyond THE RANGE.[62]

Chowbokiana reflects perhaps more disappointment than strictly accurate observation, but it is interesting as an indication of what many people must have been coming to think about New Zealand at the time. Against it may be set the opinions formed from close and continuing association with the country. L. G. D. Acland remarks in his second edition of *The Early Canterbury Runs:*

In revising my book for this edition I have read it right through and find it leaves an impression that station life in the old days was a dreary mixture of tussocks and sheep, overwhelming snowstorms and dangerous rivers; a life of tea, mutton and damper [dough baked in ashes] now and then relieved by whisky and square gin, but it wasn't as bad as that. There were many stations where people lived pleasanter, more civilized lives than most of us are likely to do in the future; stations where there was good cooking, good conversation, sound wine and pleasant company, and pretty drawing rooms where ladies played and sang.[63]

What he says is borne out by what Lady Barker was to say of her own and other station homes in *Station Life in New Zealand.* No ladies played and sang in a pretty drawing room at Mesopotamia, but they did so in country places accessible to it as well as in Christchurch.

Writing came naturally to the men in early Canterbury, fresh from college as many of them were. They kept station diaries (combined chronicles and account books), some of them personal journals besides, and, like Butler, they wrote good letters "Home." They contributed to *The Press* or other local papers. Moreover, they became parents of writers. Some of them in their later years wrote and published their reminiscences, or gave information gladly and carefully to younger generations of historians. All of them made up the audience for the local writer—fit audience though few. Butler speaks flippantly if he means in *A First Year* that it will not do to propose cultural matters to his neighbors for discussion; more likely than not he is speaking of his own shepherds and station hands, and even then it was hardly safe to write off a manager or a cadet as a-literate. In the words of a contemporary Wellingtonian, "The Canterbury emigrants consider themselves rather a select circle, rather uppercrust people. In fact, some say Canterbury is rather silver-forky in character, rather inclined to clip sheep in kid gloves."[64]

On the other hand there were of course the Chowboks and the Catons. A story about a Gaelic shepherd at Anama Station, as told by Acland, reveals how, occasionally, a fugitive from justice might show up. McAuley, the shepherd, arrived speaking only Scotch Gaelic; but though his knowledge of English (which he began picking up) remained scanty, he knew sheep well enough to be considered a first-rate man.

One morning before breakfast the manager was walking down to the stable to see the shepherds, and a friend of the Peters from Scotland who was staying at Anama happened to go with him. As soon as McAuley caught sight of the visitor he disappeared, and could not be found all day. The manager found him in the hut late that night, and asked him what in the world he had been doing. "Iss he gone?" asked McAuley nervously. "Who?" asked the manager. "T'at shentleman, Mr. Brown; he iss after me!" "Nonsense, man; he's never heard of you. Why should he be after you?" McAuley said that one night he had been poaching in Brown's loch in Scotland and that Brown and his water bailiff had chased him. McAuley had the faster boat, but it was getting near daylight, so he ran ashore, picked up a stone, and "kilt ta water bailey," as he said, and left for New Zealand. "Now ta shentleman has come here after me." The manager asked Brown about it. Brown roared with laughter. The water bailiff had only been stunned.[65]

Inwardly, Butler's life at Mesopotamia was less serene than his outward demeanor and his rising prosperity might suggest. His religious doubts deepened and were confirmed, and his case against the church (and against his father as its representative) was developed further. Among his New Zealand neighbors and associates he earned a reputation for freethinking, perhaps not too difficult to acquire in a settle-

52

ment founded by the Church of England, and took time to think out his objections to dogma, which saw light immediately after his return to England in the pamphlet called *The Evidence for the Resurrection of Jesus Christ as Contained in the Four Evangelists Critically Examined* (1865) and which are imbedded in the irony of *The Fair Haven* (1873). Appropriately, the manuscript of *The Fair Haven* was deposited at Christchurch after Butler's death. In the 1860's, his religious ideas were too heterodox to commend him to Edward Chudleigh, who nevertheless admired him as a man. The extent to which he must have aired his views and attracted attention by doing so may be gauged from an anecdote related by Oliver Duff:

I was told this story by the late John Hardcastle of Timaru, whose father had a farm near the Rangitata. He was sent as a boy to get a horse shod, and when he reached the smithy, saw a stranger leading a horse away and the blacksmith standing in the door watching. As soon as the stranger was out of hearing the blacksmith said: "See 'im? 'E don't believe in Gawd!" The stranger's name was Samuel Butler.[66]

The whole society, Christchurch included, was a microcosm. In South Canterbury (the region above Otago and below the Ashburton River), not including Christchurch, a list of "Occupations in 1861" gives the following picture: beginning with 187 laborers and 151 domestic servants, there followed 99 shepherds, 66 stockowners, 59 sawyers and bushmen, 47 bullock-drivers, 35 "other station hands" and the same number also of carpenters and builders and "gentlemen," 29 overseers (fewer than half the stockowners, apparently, could afford overseers), 19 publicans, 11 mariners, 7 storekeepers, and the rest not more than 5 each—e.g., 5 medical practitioners, 2 engineers, 2 policemen, 2 teachers, 1 legal practitioner, etc. Butler was undoubtedly one of the 66 stockowners and as such was a member of the local aristocracy. He moved with comparatively little difficulty from his comfortable if very simple habitation into the parlors of his friends, and he made enough impression to be included now and then in their reminiscences.

One of the nearest-contemporary portraits of Butler appears in Kennaway's *Crusts*, where the story of the race with Caton is recounted with embellishments* and where Butler appears in a satirical poem as one of the three suitors for the attentions of the same young lady, the three being identified as "Cotton Roley," "Thomas Pellit," and "Samuel Cutler"—"all three good friends of ours, good colonists, and gentlemen," the author quickly assures the reader.[67] Of "Cutler" he states,

The second was an explorer, who had seen some very hard times, and who, inside a sunburnt and wrinkled forehead, possessed far-thinking and acute brains, and for whom all sorts of forms of deeper modern thought had much attraction. He held exposed but extensive country on the upper Rangitata, (some forty miles behind our Harketeré run) named from its river-boundaries "Mesopotamia."[68]

The poet of "A Peculiar Dream" imagines himself by a cottage in a "sea-bounded valley" where, loitering by the gate, he meets first Roley and next Cutler:

A little further on I strayed—
My dream, observe, is getting subtler—
With visage burnt, Scotch cap and all,
Whom should I meet, but Samuel Cutler.

"Gad zooks!" said I, "not at the Club?
Or safe at home with your sheep pens, O?"
"No!" he replied, "I took a stroll
To clear my brains of that Celenso."

* In *Crusts* Butler is called "Whiffler" and given credit for a "ruse" to save the day: When his rival threatens to overtake him, Whiffler dismounts, bandages his horse's leg to cause him to limp, and plods along. At length the other man overtakes him, expresses "voluble sympathy" and rides easily away, now confident of victory. As soon as he is out of sight, Whiffler remounts and flanks him by a short cut, arriving just as the Land Office is closing but in time to enter his name. Next morning his rival is dumbfounded to see himself precluded. "Whiffler was a lucky fellow," adds Kennaway, "for he afterwards let that run for a thousand a year."—*Op. cit.*, pp. 83–86.

Next is encountered a "maiden," who asks if the poet has seen her "brothers" (later changed to "cousins"), whom she describes:

> And one is burnt like black pine wood
> Bronzed in a bushman's fire;
> His forehead, when he frowns, is like
> A coil of fencing wire.
>
> His beard is black, and black his hair;
> His hat I used to carry—
> It was sometimes, I recollect,
> A very small Glengarry.

He tells her that they have not come—that

> One waits a friend—and one is mad—
> And one is on a muster.

One by one he surprises the friends as they come up to pay their respects to the young lady:

> Cutler came on, his face lit up,
> "My own, my life!" exclaiming;
> I rather turned the point of this,
> *Myself* the welcome claiming.
>
> It was too bad, I will allow,
> To break such hearts asunder;
> But I cannot answer for my dreams,
> So cease, I beg, to wonder.
>
> Cutler—as from a leafy shade
> I stept—assumed the bearing,
> The cool calm bearing that he wears
> In the very midst of shearing.
>
> He raised his hat (he's lately bought
> A hat that does him honor),
> Politely smiled upon his love,
> And—vanished round the corner.

After a similar scene with "Pellit," the maiden goes home to her cottage and the poet overtakes the three swains walking slowly along. He says to them:

> Perish my hopes!—I thought that you
> Mesopotamian squatters,
> And dwellers where the Ashburton
> O'er shingle runs and potters,
>
> Were all above that sort of thing
> On Rangitata Upper;
> Or if poetic dreams were yours,
> You only thought of Tupper.

He advises them to go home "and get on with your shearing."[69]

At shearing, Butler was no doubt on hand to help them "get on," but as things grew easier it was possible for him to be away some or even much of the time. If what Canterbury had to offer was not London or Cambridge or even Langar, it was still not so bad. We are made aware of this through the character of the young cadet who becomes the hero of *Erewhon*—if, properly speaking, the book can be said to have a hero. Physically he is robust, ready for nearly any sort of contingency and well versed in the ways of high-country life. He has learned the business of sheep farming thoroughly enough to hanker after a run of his own—something not at all out of reach in so youthful and opportunistic a country—and understands the process by which he can most easily hope to obtain it. Intellectually he has been dampered down to suit certain of Butler's satiric purposes, but he is no fool. His principal eccentricities and absurdities are religious, suited to the mood of rejection uncommonly strong in Butler's New Zealand years and for some years following. He handles himself well enough through the ordeal of penetrating into Erewhon, after which he tends to dissipate through a long middle-section Erewhonian fantasia, to reappear briefly during the escape scene and in the conclusion. All in all, he is probably a good deal like Samuel Butler—a hardier (and foolhardier) person than the author of *Erewhon,* but recalled with a limited measure of sound satisfaction. Mesopotamia produced such a character, first in reality and later in retrospective imagination. And for Butler, Christchurch held even more.

CHRISTCHURCH

We shake our dear old England by the hand
And watch space dwindling, while the shrinking
world
Collapses into nothing. Mark me well,
Matter as swift as swiftest thought shall fly,
And space itself be nowhere . . .

THE ENGLISH CRICKETERS

Mesopotamia itself was not quite a primitivistic paradise, even in periods of comparative solitude, which were not so frequent or prolonged as has been imagined. Interpretations of Butler's New Zealand residence which rest on premises like those of Paul Elmer More (and his premises are fairly typical) are not in possession of the facts. "It must be remembered," says More, "that Butler wrote this essay ["Darwin Among the Machines"] while living in the free primitive uplands of New Zealand, during the happiest period of his life, and that the note of primitivism in his peroration is probably in large measure sincere."[1] Or, again, "It is scarcely too much to say that all the product of his later life was the fruit of this period of quiet incubation."[2] It was a period of incubation, to be sure, and much (if somewhat less than "all") of the product of his later life was the fruit of it. Of the "quiet," however, one is not so sure. Those who imagine the frontier an ideal place for "quiet incubation" in all likelihood have never lived there.

And in any event Butler by no means spent all his time at Mesopotamia; there were long periods of residence in town. The "metropolis" of Christchurch can hardly be considered a literal parallel to the towns of Erewhon, but it did provide the Canterbury Settlement with clear-cut elements of contrast to the surrounding sheep country, just as in *Erewhon* itself we are rather quickly and totally involved with town-bred people and town-bred ways, once the romantic preliminaries are past. Physically the Erewhonians are presented as a glorified peasantry, but their behavior and their problems are too elaborately social, too essentially urban, to be typical of country folk. They are, in short, the people Butler most generally associated with, if not necessarily the ones with whom he felt most at ease. One set of ideas, thus—the poetic response to the mountains so evident in *Erewhon*—Butler may well have developed and matured at Mesopotamia, but there were others that involved more than solitude: the question of man and machinery, the paralyzing effects of ecclesiasticism, the absurdities only too evident in education, the pitiless estrangement of ill-suited parent and child. The self-important little city on New Zealand's Avon was a reminder that all the old institutions still existed.

To Christchurch—as the seat of government, the link with "Home," the base of supplies—the squatters came with frequency and often stayed for considerable lengths of time. A man of substance not immediately involved in the arduous business of setting up a station could delegate management to an overseer and become, in a small way, a counterpart of the English squire who spent seasons in "the town." Though obviously no metropolis as yet, Christchurch-on-Avon was developing its attractions.

Such attractions as it afforded were intended as only a slightly reconstituted extension of British life; naturally its founders would have called the place "Christchurch"—or something equally Anglo-Saxon. The name may have been from Christchurch College, Oxford, or from

Christchurch in Hampshire, where there is an Avon River; opinion is divided. And although there was once a proposal to name the new settlement Stratford, the Avon River of Christchurch appears to have been named after the Avon in Lanarkshire, not Warwickshire.[3] But there is no question about the colonists' desire to make Christchurch their antipodean "Home"; that New Zealand was on the other side of the earth, under different heavens and in a different hemisphere, was in their minds strictly incidental. British tenacity would see to it that there was no succumbing to nonsense from wild colonial boys as in Australia or—worse—to "Americanisation" (which was really what ailed Australia).

But prim as it intended itself to be, Christchurch never became as dour as Dunedin, the Presbyterian settlement to the southward, destined (with Christchurch) to be one of the two principal centers of South Island. Crosbie Ward in 1857 described Christchurch as

> . . . an elegant mixture
> Of roads and pasture
>   And swamp and sand;
> So widely stretching
> In each direction,
> From Brittan's section
>   To Caulfield's land,

going on to say,

> Oh! fifty twenties
> The whole extent is
> Of English acres,
>   All in a square;
> And plenty of space is
> In the vacant places,
> With patches of praties
>   Lying here and there.[4]

Another poem of 1860 (not by Ward), "Growl in a Sou'wester," is even less flattering:

Christchurch

Land where men with brains of fog
Built a city in a bog!
Land of rain, and storm, and flood!
Land of water, wind, and mud!
Where six days a week the gale,
Laden thick with rain or hail,
First from sou'-west blows a piercer,
Then veers nor'-west and blows fiercer!
   This is what I think of thee,
   Eden of the Southern Sea.[5]

The very presence of Crosbie Ward, and others of his stripe, is significant, both for Christchurch itself and for the stimulus such men afforded Butler. Ten years later, when Ward departed for England as agent of the Provincial government, he was given a public dinner.[6] Christchurch liked a man of intelligence with literary pretensions, for the reason that all the leading citizens were men of intelligence and not a few had literary abilities if not pretensions. Until quite recent years, the story of literature in New Zealand has been one of potential talents too often submerged in practical affairs—the usual pattern in new areas.

No pioneering community can be the acme of comfort, but New Zealand tried. Even the missionaries brought out to North Island, in the 1820's, such personal comforts as hand-painted plates, ivory fans, silver pencils, Chinese tea-caddies, and books of music—some of these acquired in India en route, no doubt. The Rev. Richard Davis, arriving in 1823, carried with him to accompany hymn tunes a flute, which must have interested his Maori converts who so lately had made their own flutes from their enemies' arm bones. Sometimes a wooden "tuning whistle" about a foot long was used to start the singing. In the Rev. Mr. Davis' church a deep pottery bowl profusely ornamented with blue floral designs served as the baptismal font. Young ladies worked samplers such as one reading: "Lost—Somewhere between sunrise and sunset—TWO GOLDEN HOURS—Each set with sixty Diamond Minutes—No reward is offered for they are LOST FOR

EVER—Work while it is day for the night cometh when no man works." Ernest Pontifex' start at organ-building in *The Way of All Flesh* is paralleled (and considerably outdone) by the feat of William Webster, owner of timber-, flour-, and flax-mills at Hokianga (north of Auckland), who in 1850 completed a pipe organ built during his spare time: two metal stops came from England, two wooden ones were hand-sawn; the ivory keyboard was of sperm whales' teeth, the black keys colored by a Maori dye; all the iron and brass work was hand-wrought; the outside case was of Australian cedar. This instrument, to be seen in the Auckland Old Colonists Museum, was used every Sunday for home services attended by neighbors and is still in playing condition. Seeing that he carted his own piano to Mesopotamia, Butler would probably have thought that William Webster was better occupied at his organ-building than the young ladies at their samplers, though both activities probably fulfilled a creative urge. The pianos commonly brought out were about the size of a modern spinet or slightly smaller, especially if they were to be freighted by bullock dray or (in North Island) by small river craft.

All this came about through the water link with Britain, which served to make possible and to promote quickly a surprising display of social elegance. Fashionable dresses, furniture, books, and other "luxuries," which in less favorably situated communities might be many years in appearing, were sent out by ship at not too exorbitant a rate for the prosperous colonists to afford, though then as now distance inevitably influenced price. The Canterbury Pilgrims brought enough money with them to justify early shopkeeping, and in nearly every particular they were quite the reverse, economically speaking, of that earlier band of Pilgrims who landed at Plymouth Rock in the age of the first Samuel Butler. They had not been in Canterbury for a full year when there was a meeting to consider forming a Canterbury Jockey Club.[7]

Twelve years previous to the publication of *Erewhon,* then, Butler was arriving at a frontier town that was barely ten years old; and yet ten years was enough to soften the earlier rawness, just as that short a time (or usually less) had served to bring many of the sheep stations to a more than tolerable state of comfort. When Sir George Grey returned to Canterbury in 1867 (he had been there sixteen years before), he said he felt like Rip Van Winkle, things had changed so bewilderingly. Sir George assisted further the process of change by presenting the people of Canterbury with a pair of silver-gray rabbits whose progeny, or at any rate whose later congeners, were destined to eat the sheep farmers out of house and home.[8] But as of 1860 and for some time to come, the place was still rough around the edges: the streets were muddy, most of the buildings were unsubstantial wooden structures, the river banks were unkempt, as were most of the tracts of public land (Christchurch, like most cities in New Zealand, had fore-sightedly reserved "green belt" properties as parks) and many private holdings. There were wide and somewhat desolate-looking spaces between buildings, with an occasional patch of "praties" or cabbages or other vegetables. Henry Sewell, a contemporary observer, described the approach to the wooden Provincial Council Chambers in these depressing terms: "The externals are shabby in the extreme—a low, desolate looking wooden tenement, all by itself in a potato garden, a quarter of a mile at least from the inhabited part of town, approached on an open trackless common covered with fern and tussock grass, barely passable in dry weather and miserable in wet." Sewell found the expense of living "about double that of London, with one-fourth part of the comfort."[9] This was in 1853; not many years later an anonymous poet paid tribute to both the Provincial Council Chambers and its occupants in these verses:

> Solemn Body! Sacred Spot!
>   Lukewarm; neither cold nor hot.
> Clerk, half nodding, drops a blot.
>   Opposition talking rot,
> How the country goes to pot.
>   Government regarding not,
> Driving on their old jog trot.
>   Members, independent lot,

63

Sitting, caring not a jot;
Voting, for they know not what,
Money that they haven't got.
Solemn Body! Sacred Spot![10]

The yucca-like Maori flax, *Phormium tenax,* grew rank in damp places, and, aggravating the situation, the settlers themselves had introduced watercress into the Avon and Heathcote, so that by 1857 the Provincial Council was obliged to spend £1,500 in an attempt to clear the rivers. "Undeterred by this experience," says Wigram, "some enthusiastic fishermen subsequently introduced an even worse pest—the American water-weed—which it was expected would harbour food for trout."[11] And, undeterred by Nature's botanical warning, the sportsmen had to have their deer and rabbits, which became the worst problems of all. The late Herbert Guthrie-Smith, New Zealand's most distinguished naturalist, indignantly observes that "so far the best that has been done towards the conservation of species is but negative. At the best, man has here and there been content not to destroy utterly."[12] He points out in another place that all the animals ever introduced into New Zealand, with the exception of rainbow trout, have become pests.

But the presence of game marked the presence of gentlemen, who were coming in a steady stream. In April, 1854, Sewell chronicled the arrival of John Cracroft Wilson:

> In the evening a new arrival, the "Ackbar," from Sydney, bringing Mr. Wilson, an Indian with a retinue of coolies, and intended to bring all sorts of animals, antelopes, hares, deer, etc., but unhappily, most of them died on the voyage. . . .
>
> I am sadly afraid that the Indian Nabob will be grievously disgusted, and carry back evil reports to India, whither he is to return.[13]

In view of subsequent developments, "unhappily" is perhaps not quite the best word: had they survived to be turned loose and breed, most of the animals would shortly have become nuisances. But a more significant point is that the "Nabob"—already in 1854—had the notion that Canterbury was the ideal place of retirement; and in fact many who were retired from the Indian Service did come on down to New Zealand.

In the formative years there was (as in nearly all new settlements) a strong "one big family" spirit among the colonists. They joked about their mutual hardships, told stories on each other, and strove hard to keep themselves reminded of the better days ahead. Humor, as a necessary article of pioneer equipment, was a part of their makeup. And with town and country so closely allied, the broad joke was popular everywhere. For example:

One of the people who lived at Arowhenua in the early days was an inveterate practical joker. A man had been drowned in the river there, and during the inquest at the Accommodation House, while the Coroner and a jury were having lunch, the practical joker removed the corpse and got into its place, and when they lifted the sheet to view the body, he greeted them with loud guffaws.[14]

There were "characters" whose eccentricities made good conversation, such as "Honest John Cordy," of whom it was reported, "when he first came over the Bridle Path he met a Maori, and neither knew what to make of the other, but Cordy tried to put things right by shouting 'I'm honest John Cordy from Suffolk. Is it peace or war? Is it peace or war?' "[15]

Charles George Tripp, one of the high-country settlers (for a time, Butler's neighbor at Mt. Peel) and "a curious mixture of simplicity and shrewdness," was "so full of energy that he could hardly sit through his meals, and often said grace as he ran from the door to the dining table."[16]

Once, while they were crossing the Rangitata, Mrs. Tripp was washed down the river in a boat, and Tripp found himself unable to get to her assistance. He is said to have shouted from the bank: "Goodbye, Ellen, goodbye, meet you in Heaven you know, meet you in Heaven."[17]

"More stories," says Acland, "were told of him in shearers' huts and mustering camps than of any runholder in Canterbury." No wonder!

65

Christchurch itself could show here and there an oddity, as for example George Willmer, the occasional-poet described by Johannes Andersen:

A most constant visitor to our mapping-room during my early years there was a man whom many folks will remember—old George Willmer. As everybody knows, he used to drive cattle, he used to play cricket with the veterans, and he used to write poetry. He wrote to celebrate all kinds of occasions—jubilees, opening of bridges, installations of Governors, laying of foundation stones, shipwrecks, colliery disasters. The effusions were not long; usually they were commendably brief. Generally they could be, and were printed on small cards, coloured in some pale tint, green or blue or yellow, usually with ornamental border. He would come into the office with a smiling "Good-morning, gentlemen," and one of these cards held between his forefinger and middle finger and with his genial greeting extract shillings in exchange for cards. . . . Good old Willmer, with his grey beard, and his limp, and his smile, and his "Well, gentlemen, how are we this day of jubilee?"[18]

And mingled with the George Willmers were men of real talent. Christchurch, with a population of three thousand, was well up to the standard set forth in Butler's *Note-Books*:

Bravery, wit and poetry abound in every village. . . . There is not a village of 500 inhabitants in England but has its Mrs. Quickly and its Tom Jones. These good people never understand themselves, they go over their own heads, they speak in an unknown tongue to those around them and the interpreter is the rarer and more important person. The *vates sacer* is the middleman of mind.[19]

Butler left just a year too early to have been a contributor to *Canterbury Punch*, which ran from April to August, 1865. He did his part, however, in one local collection called *Literary Foundlings*, published in 1864 as a benefit for an orphan's home: "A Note on *The Tempest*, Act III, Scene I."[20] A light spoof at Shakespeare and the colony as well, it makes Ferdinand out as a back-country cadet who has been set the task of gathering firewood from the bush—a fragment of Shakespeare-in-modern-dress, the dress in this instance being New Zealand colonial. Canterbury was a place where wit was esteemed and freely indulged, both in public and in private. The light verse of Crosbie Ward, for some years editor of the *Lyttelton Times,* was the most frequent and consistently the best.

The growth of Christchurch was steady during Butler's sojourn in New Zealand, as was also the process of amelioration in its physical arrangements. Sir George Grey meant what he said about his Rip Van Winkle impressions; and even so short a residence as five years saw many changes. Butler could almost have said that he found Christchurch in wood, and left, or was leaving, it in limestone: at the time of his departure in June, 1864, many marks of permanence were appearing, such as a new stone bridge under construction at a cost of £3,000 to replace a wooden structure costing slightly under £300.[21] A new town hall of stone had already been completed, as had a portion of the permanent Provincial Council Chambers and a new clubhouse for the Christchurch Club. Shops were increasing in number and in elegance; there were new hotels, new livery stables, and a variety of entertainment savoring strongly of prosperity.

For the most part the entertainers were fresh from Australia, making the side trip to New Zealand before returning "Home" or possibly going on to California. If in June of 1864 Butler had cared to divert himself before departing, as perhaps he did, he would have had his choice of Kohler's Gardens, where there were quadrille assemblies, public and private dinners, "band always in attendance," and "magnificent statuary on view"; or the Royal Princess' Theatre, then featuring "the eminent Irish Comedian Mr. Shiel Barry in two Hibernian characters, Handy Andy, and O'Callaghan on His Last Legs"; or the Town Hall, with a "grand exhibition of living wonders consisting of the Bearded Lady and her son, Young Esau, the Bearded Boy, also the Swiss Warbler, a wonderful imitator of birds and animals"; or finally, the Wheel of Fortune at the Canterbury Fancy Bazaar (J. Josephs, Prop.), offering such prizes as glove boxes, concertinas, dressing cases, electro-plated cruet frames, and "a variety of other useful and ornamental articles too numerous to particularise. . . . As there are no blanks, YOU MUST GET A PRIZE."[22]

Theater fare was meagre enough, since bringing a company to New Zealand for the limited opportunities of performance was financially unsound, but concert parties and itinerant solo artists showed up with some regularity. One such soloist was Shiel Barry; another the comedian Thatcher. Especially good at improvising on local themes, Thatcher—who was in Christchurch during August of 1862—found himself at odds with a local lawyer, W. T. L. Travers, who took umbrage at something Thatcher had said of him and denounced the singer in the *Lyttelton Times* as an impostor and traveling mountebank. Thatcher replied, using a verse pattern borrowed from Lowell's *Biglow Papers,*

> Travers to Thatcher's concert repairs,
>   Is noticed in song, and it dreadfully riles him,
> To give him a slight rub the vocalist dares,
>   And the lawyer a "travelling mountebank" styles him,
>   But W. T.
>   Locke Travers he
> Don't do justice to *Slaters* and *Thatchers* you see.[23]

Transportation was slowly emerging from the horseback and bullock-cart stage, though to the high country the innovations on the plains and elsewhere were to make comparatively little difference. But the famous "Cobb and Co." stagecoaches had established themselves in 1863 and the first hansom cab appeared in Christchurch in 1864. Like the reconstructed Erewhonians of *Erewhon Revisited,* the Christchurchians "repealed" the laws—i.e., the natural limitations—against machinery. All this was instructive to contemplate; it recapitulated, within a very brief span of years, the technological progress of virtually the whole century just past, which had taken Europe from mud ruts to iron rails.

The most difficult, expensive, and sensational development was the Christchurch-Lyttelton tunnel, bored through the Port Hills to accommodate a railway line. Because of the height and steepness of the hills, communication between Lyttelton and Christchurch was tedious, not to mention its cost. A tunnel and short railway would solve the problem. But serious contemplation of such an undertaking took public spirit of a transcendent kind—even more than could be generated by the local Chamber of Commerce, which began at Lyttelton in 1859 and moved to Christchurch in 1863 (the move itself a testimony to the growing importance of the metropolis-to-be). Quick transmission of news had already been assured by a telegraph line between the two towns (first operated on July 1, 1862), which enabled dispatches from incoming ships to reach Christchurch in a matter of minutes—market reports, in all likelihood, being the most urgently desired. Rapidly enough, man the "machinate animal" (as *Erewhon* puts it) was growing supplementary limbs, "extra-corporeal members, which are of more importance to him than a good deal of his hair, or at any rate than his whiskers."[24] As squatter and townsman by turns, the author of *Erewhon* was aware of all this both as spectator and as participant. The railroad project, typical of colonial exuberance and yet in its way a heroic chapter in the life of the province, was soon to offer him food for reflection. And since it was even to involve him personally—slightly enough, but quite palpably—the story bears retelling in some detail.

To the pioneer, "extra-corporeal members" appealed with special force; chained to a bullock dray, he could readily sense the accretion of power that came with a railway or even with something so modest as a bridge or an all-weather road. Some pioneers, while not questioning the desirability of change, are cautious about trying to provide new developments too soon. Others—and they are rather typical on frontiers—put their full force behind agitation for improvement which they feel must justify itself financially, once achieved. Such a man was Butler's friend William Sefton Moorhouse, whom he described in later life as "one of the very finest men whose path I ever crossed." Moorhouse, a man of great personal charm and public devotion, was the second elected superintendent of the Province and (after the days of

69

Edward Gibbon Wakefield and until the days of Julius Vogel) the most energetic promoter in New Zealand. Although Butler could laugh at him for imagining himself being converted to Christianity "by reading Burton's *Anatomy of Melancholy,* which he had got by mistake for [Bishop] Butler's *Analogy,* on the recommendation of a friend," he admired him tremendously for his forthrightness, honesty, and practicality, cardinal Butlerian virtues as well as assets in a country still to be developed. One of his favorite sayings, recalled in the *Note-Books,* is typical: "Men cannot get rich by swopping knives." Canterbury would prosper, Moorhouse was convinced, only through willingness to take a few calculated risks.[25]

Moorhouse, properly speaking, was a "Prophet": with his two younger brothers he had spent several years in Australia, where he had imbibed more heady draughts of the philosophy of progress than had some of the "Pilgrims." All the Moorhouses, says Booth, were "exceedingly fine men over six feet in height and built in proportion, good shots and experts at most games of strength and skill."[26] William Sefton Moorhouse was possessed of ideas to match his physique; and in the contest about to be waged with James Edward Fitzgerald, he became the brawny incarnation of colonial enterprise as against the sort of "home-bred" conservatism which still serves in a measure to distinguish Australia from New Zealand.

When first elected superintendent in 1857 (after campaigning as "the working-man's friend"), Moorhouse had not yet become interested in the tunnel project; but as the result of agitation by the *Lyttelton Times* and individual citizens, the Provincial Council late in 1858 set about collecting information through the Provincial engineer E. Dobson. Three commissioners were appointed to further the cause in London, James Edward Fitzgerald (then emigration officer there) being one. Fitzgerald, who had taken with him to London a geographical model of the Port Hills, was unenthusiastic; he believed that a high-level railway, using American techniques, would be better than a tunnel. The commission submitted the problem to the engineer Robert Stephenson, then in his declining years, who referred it to George Robert Stephenson. The younger Stephenson, after considering three alternate routes (including the high-level one), reported on August 10, 1859, that the tunnel scheme seemed best to him. He thought the work could be done for £250,000. (This was approximately six weeks before Butler sailed for New Zealand.) Thereupon, the commissioners asked him to find them a contractor and he recommended "Smith, Knight and Co.," who offered to do the work for £235,000. In December the Provincial Council, after long and serious debate, passed two bills enabling the work to begin but providing only a portion of the necessary finances. Public sentiment was strong for the project. There was official hesitation, however, and when at length the Provincial Council's bills were vetoed by the governor (the chief officer of New Zealand, superior to the Provincial Council), a public meeting in Christchurch sent endorsement to the General Assembly then meeting at Auckland. In July, 1860, the General Assembly authorized the Provincial Council to pass a loan bill for as much as £200,000, and work began.

But new obstacles arose: the contractor, having encountered some uncommonly hard stone in the volcanic hills, decided that he could not carry on. In November he repudiated his contract and went home. December was a critical month, calling for all of Moorhouse's strength of will and possibly a little more. One contractor had already given up and it was not likely that another could easily be found. Crosbie Ward was on hand with another parody of Longfellow:

> Provincial funds were falling fast,
> When to the Council Chamber passed
> A man who held with red tape tied,
> A paper, with these words outside,
> "Railroadior."
>
> .   .   .   .   .   .
>
> "Try not the tunnel," old hands said,
> "Loose hang the boulders overhead,

71

Mesopotamian Squatter

"The work is long, the cost is high;"
"Hang the expense" was his reply,
"Railroadior."[27]

At this point Dr. Julius Haast came into the picture. Haast, already a geologist of reputation, was engaged to survey prospects, and reported on December 20, 1860, that the hard rock was not present in large quantity and that the bulk of the tunnel would be easy going; that in his opinion the tunnel might even be completed sooner and for less money than first estimates had indicated. Accordingly, in early January, Moorhouse was instructed to find another contractor. This time he turned to Australia, and at Melbourne in mid-April, 1861, entered a provisional contract with "Holmes & Co." and also floated a loan of £300,000. Returning with Holmes in late April, he found public support still strong. The contract bid was set at £240,500 and the loan confirmed on May 16. E. Richardson, Holmes's partner, arrived to take charge and work got under way again on July 17 with a sod-turning and banquet. Swopping contractors, fortunately, was to prove better than swopping knives.

A little belatedly, Fitzgerald, still unconvinced, founded the Christchurch *Press* and began publishing on May 25, 1861, with the intention of continuing his opposition. As a friend to both Moorhouse and Fitzgerald, Butler was in the midst of this political cross fire, but he seems to have kept out of serious personal involvement—not too easy a task for him in his later years. Both men no doubt appealed to him very strongly: Fitzgerald, the intellectual leader of men in a strongly intellectual society—highly capable, well-educated (B.A. at Christ's College, Cambridge, in 1842), a gentleman and scholar; Moorhouse, gifted at practicalities, a reader of Thackeray and Dickens in preference to the classics, never wealthy and in fact often in debt, a genial politician and moreover an honest one. These were but two out of a circle of choice acquaintances.

"Community of limbs," says *Erewhon,* is possible to "those who have so much community of soul as to own money enough to pay a rail-

72

way fare; for a train is only a seven leagued foot that five hundred may own at once."[28] With singular "community of soul" the colonists embraced their railway project, and their glad acceptance must have afforded Butler much food for speculation on the power and influence of machinery upon society. He was in the right place to see it.

Rather than wait for completion of the tunnel, Moorhouse went ahead to provide a stop-gap arrangement in the form of a short branch railway from Christchurch to Ferrymead, on the estuary of the Avon-Heathcote rivers. Chiefly, this was to save the wearisome draying of goods unloaded from ships at Lyttelton and brought around the heads in small craft to shallower water. But it must also have occurred to Moorhouse that his larger project would retain support more easily if a segment of railway was already a going concern. For these reasons, the Ferrymead railway was constructed concurrently with the tunnel-driving and was completed late in 1863, some four years before the opening of the tunnel. The event was successful enough to give "Railroadior" and his friends a foretaste of triumph: by this time, it was apparent to everybody that Moorhouse had won.

The festivities celebrating the opening of the Ferrymead line involved Butler, both by special invitation and by unexpected solicitation. In a mood of reminiscence early in 1902 Butler recalled:

I suppose I am probably the last survivor of those who rode on the trial trip of the first locomotive that ever travelled in New Zealand. Moorhouse, Reeves, myself and one other (but of this I am not certain) were the only ones on the engine as it started from Christchurch and ran to the Heathcote.[29]

The ceremonies were held on the afternoon of Tuesday, December 1, 1863, with a nor'wester blowing dust amidst summer heat (Monday night had threatened rain). The time for the first train to run had been set for 1:30, but the superintendent of the Province, Mr. Bealey, was late arriving (one of his team of four gray horses had become refractory, a newspaper account reported). The first trainload, which contained "few passengers but those connected with the Government and

The railway opening, as drawn for the *Illustrated London News*

Illustrated London News

members of the Provincial Council," pulled out at 2:03 and "soon quickening into a pretty fast pace, landed its contents without the least interruption at Ferrymead at 2:13 P.M. exactly."* Railroad time was already making itself felt in Canterbury. Neither the account in the *Press* nor the one in the *Lyttelton Times,* understandably enough, mentions the detail that Samuel Butler was on the engine, but the *Press* had some words for Moorhouse:

> We observed Mr. Moorhouse standing on the engine, with an air almost of severity upon his features. We noticed that as the train passed the platform he did not move a muscle in his countenance; neither did he lift from his head that shabby dusty hat with which we are all so familiar, until a vociferous cheer greeted him from the masses; but before the sound of the cheer had reached him his face had unbent, his hat was off his head, and he seemed for the first time to feel himself at home. The trait is too characteristic to be passed without notice.[30]

After the first trip had been made, there was a free-for-all series of rides extending into twilight and accommodating some thirty-five hundred people. It was a red-letter day for promoters and populace alike; many of the colonists had never seen a railway train.

The banquet, a "really magnificent *dejeuner,*" the *Press* termed it, was served in the freight shed at Ferrymead. There was champagne, a band, and all the trimmings—flags, evergreen foliage on the pillars, ornamental festoons of blue calico, and mottoes: "God Save the Queen," "Success to the Lyttelton and Christchurch Railway," "Railways and Progress," "Advance Canterbury." Two long tables were insufficient for the crowd. It is not clear whether all five hundred of the invited guests were at the tables or whether it was first come, first served; at any rate, as the *Lyttelton Times* reported it:

> Perhaps the most amusing part of the proceedings were the picnician makeshifts of those who were unable to procure seats at the tables; down one side of the shed a row of waggons were placed, some were covered

---

* The distance from Ferrymead to Christchurch was four miles, twenty-nine chains; the average speed of the train, 25.7 miles per hour.

over to do duty as sideboards, others were empty, into these later incontinently went the unseated, and, arranged in groups, catered for themselves. We saw one party of nine, amongst whom there were only three knives, one of them being a carver, and two forks. We saw one gentleman insanely attempting to carve a ham with a penknife no bigger than a knitting needle; another demolishing a fowl in a very primitive manner; but notwithstanding all these drawbacks, it is a strange fact that the choicest dishes accumulated in a most mysterious manner round these apparently outsiders.[31]

There was a band, which played "Come Where My Love Lies Dreaming" and "other airs, with good effect," including one called "Cheer Up Sam"—not for Samuel Butler but for Samuel Bealey, superintendent of the Province, whose speech followed the toast to the Queen. After a brief speech by Mr. John Ollivier ("Oloware the fluent" of Ward's "Song of the Squatters") there was a toast to the health of the Lyttelton City Council (all the speeches were in response to toasts).

Moorhouse's speech, the *pièce de résistance,* was an epitome of the colonial philosophy of progress. Introduced by one of the elder clergy —Archdeacon Mathias, who praised Moorhouse for his "disregard of clamorous opposition and unjust censure"—Moorhouse was given a rousing ovation. "Never did we hear the like," said the *Press,* "and, as we heard it remarked, he must be indeed a glutton for public approbation who could wish for a more marked and cordial reception."

The building regularly roared applause, and at one time it seemed doubtful whether Mr. Moorhouse would ever be allowed to begin his speech: time after time when the cheering seemed on the point of ceasing, the cry of "one cheer more" was the signal for another roar, until at length people were regularly exhausted with shouting and stamping and Mr. Moorhouse was allowed to speak.

At last, "not without reasonable agitation," Moorhouse delivered his remarks. He was happy, he said, to see the realization of his hopes. Although strongly opposed by all the "heaviest intellect of the Province" (this was a bow at Fitzgerald) and told by "all the financial acumen of Canterbury" that he was bankrupting the settlement, it was

76

now clear that what he had fought for was evident in the commence-
ment of "a new era for Canterbury." The *Press* account continues:

Favored by nature with invaluable resources we had now commenced
supplementing the development of these resources with the greatest triumph
of modern science and ingenuity, and he was not afraid to say that we had
the chances before us of attaining to the most perfect development in every
respect of any nation upon earth. We had national youth on our side, we
were not now in the decrepit old world which we had left—(oh! oh!)—
we must act in a manner worthy of youth and strength, and move forward
as it became sons of England to do. We must press on; we must never stop;
the present railway was nothing but a little experiment; by and bye we
should see further extensions; we must never rest content as long as anything is undone which is within the bounds of human possibility to achieve.
He hoped to live to see the day when a merchant should send his clerk
from Port Lyttelton to Timaru [about a hundred miles] with the injunction
to be back by tea-time (*laughter*). There was no need to laugh: what he
said would be a fact, a real, great, practical fact—and with facts of this
nature within our reach it would be impossible to stop: he was sure the
present Superintendent would go on with the good work; it was as necessary to go on as it had been to begin; all things would progress in a relative
ratio to the facilities for communication and traffic.

In a gesture toward the doubting squatterarchy, Moorhouse assured
the large sheepmen that "the pastoral interest would be as much bene-
fited as any other interest: instead of renting large tracts of wild and
unimproved land the present squatters would be owners of larger or
smaller tracts of improved freehold, and would find that they carried
more sheep by this means than by the other." ("Here," said the re-
porter, "we noticed a certain disconsolateness in one or two squatters in
the vicinity of the speaker.") In conclusion, he warned his listeners
against assuming there would be easy paternalism in the government:

If the people expected the Government to do well by them they must do
well by Government—people must not look to Government to do every
thing for them. . . . They were themselves the bone and sinews of the

Government, and unless the Government found itself backed up by energy, enterprise, and forethought on the part of the people there might as well be no Government at all, for all the good that would be done.

After Moorhouse, the contractors (Holmes & Co.) were honored, as was also Mr. Dobson, Provincial engineer, who pronounced the tunnel "the most important engineering work in the Southern Seas." A toast to the ladies was of course inevitable, but the response had not been prearranged, and Mr. A. Sheath, who was "called upon suddenly to reply" stumbled a bit in finding something appropriate to say.

Here it might be mentioned that to be asked to respond to a toast is still somewhat of a public honor in New Zealand. It is a measure of Samuel Butler's importance as a local journalist, therefore, that he was singled out for distinction—not as first choice, to be sure, but still as a man to ask for a response. The *Lyttelton Times* report is noncommittal: "Mr. J. S. Williams proposed the Press of Canterbury. The toast was received with great cheering, and was briefly acknowledged by Mr. Butler." The *Press* did a little better by Butler, but not remarkably so:

> The Press of Canterbury was then proposed, coupled with the name of Mr. Reeves. Mr. Reeves was not present, and Mr. Butler was called upon as unexpectedly as Mr. Sheath had been. He spoke in such a low tone that we could hardly hear him, but we understand that he regretted the absence of Mr. Reeves and Mr. Fitzgerald and denied all connection with the Press of Canterbury or with Mr. Samuel Butler of the Rangitata district.*

Butler's speech was almost the last, but the crowd had not yet had enough of Moorhouse:

> The assembled guests then left the shed, and proceeded to the platform to witness the arrivals and departures of the trains, filled to overflowing with the crowds of delighted excursionists. Shortly after this time a large crowd assembled in front of the entrance to the booking office, and Mr. Moorhouse being called for, was hoisted upon the roof, from which position

---

* Reeves, according to Butler's reminiscence of 1902, was on the engine, but apparently not available at the dinner.

he delivered a telling speech, which was received with great cheering, and on concluding he was carried about on the shoulders of the people.[32]

The same evening, the little ship *Gazelle,* which had brought a crowd of passengers around from Lyttelton, did its part to emphasize once more the need for a tunnel:

The *Gazelle* [reported *The Press*] left the jetty about 8 in the morning, crowded with passengers, but upon their return in the evening, they managed to get stuck fast on a mud flat, between the Ferry and Sumner, and were obliged to a return home on foot, which was rather an unpleasant termination of a day's holiday.[33]

Butler's close connection with Moorhouse, pretty clearly the most popular man in the Province ("He was a clean politician," says Andersen,[34] "and with all his chances in public life it is said he never made a shilling out of it") is evident from the invitation to ride on the engine. The man who proposed the toast to the Press of Canterbury, and probably called on Butler to reply, was Joshua Strange Williams, then a member of the Provincial Council. Another Cantabrigian (B.A. Trinity College, 1857), Williams did well enough at law in Canterbury to be appointed to the Supreme Court in 1875. Later knighted, he also served at one time as chancellor of the University of Otago; he was reputedly witty, and well-read in French and Italian.

To a young man in Butler's shoes the opportunity of knowing immediately such people as these was an immeasurable advantage. He did not need to seek association or curry favor; it was the natural order of events for him to be thrown readily into the company of the leaders, and it must have been something of a shock to be reminded, upon his return to England, that friends of influence were not so easy to come by in London.

To mention everyone of prominence Butler knew in and around Christchurch would be to recapitulate large sections of the *Dictionary of New Zealand Biography,* but there were several who were particularly close. James Edward Fitzgerald, owner of *The Press,* was, like

Williams and Rolleston, a Cambridge man. Fully deserving Moorhouse's wry compliment as the "heaviest intellect of the Province," Fitzgerald had been from the beginning of the Canterbury Settlement a major power and was to remain so, later moving to Wellington to take part in national affairs. He was much concerned over native policy (the columns of *The Press* reflect this clearly) and made several notable speeches before Parliament in behalf of the Maoris. In the Weld Ministry (1864/65) he became Minister of Native Affairs, and for more than thirty years held positions as comptroller-general or comptroller and auditor-general. Among the "nice people" Fitzgerald was in point of influence probably the very nicest.

A different set of interests, more in the direction of Darwinism, is represented in Dr. Julius Haast (who was to be knighted by both the Austrian and British governments). Haast, born in Germany, near Bonn, in 1822 (his father was a merchant and burgomeister), was educated at the University of Bonn in geology and mineralogy, and for some time traveled about Europe as a merchant, not neglecting, however, such geological opportunities as an ascent of Mt. Aetna after the eruption of 1852. He came to New Zealand in 1858 (to North Island) to report to a London firm of shipowners on the suitability of the country for emigration; his verdict must have been favorable, for he remained there the rest of his life to enjoy a very distinguished career. As Provincial geologist, Haast was based in Christchurch but spent six or eight months of every year in the field, where he first encountered Butler at Mesopotamia. A good singer and violinist, Haast loved music as much as science and was in fact a gifted amateur in all the arts. Even after Butler had returned to England, he sought Haast's opinions on his painting; they corresponded and enjoyed a reunion in 1886, when Haast came to London. Such catholicity of interests led Haast rather naturally into sponsorship of the Canterbury Museum (opened in 1870) and the Philosophical Institute.

Whether or not Haast criticized Butler's paintings while the two were together in Christchurch we do not know, but there is evidence that Butler did continue, at least occasionally, to paint: a portrait dated

1860 has survived. Others, of visiting New Zealanders done after his return to England, found their way back to the colony, e.g., one of John Marshman, who was a local official of some prominence, in the land office and in other capacities; and one of the surveyor Thomas Cass. Possibly there are other pictures from this period that have not yet come to light. One recalls that Butler tried unsuccessfully for the Slade Professorship of Art at Cambridge in 1886; with friends like Haast, Fitzgerald, and others to back him he could probably have secured a professorship at Canterbury College or the University of Otago without difficulty. Haast sent plants to Canon Butler and at one time (in 1865) had the promise of a portrait by Samuel when he could come to London.

To Frederick Napier Broome, a fellow runholder and the second husband of Lady Barker, Butler said he owed the "final shove" into *Erewhon* after both men had returned to England. Broome's later career took him to western Australia, where he was unusually successful as governor (1882–1890), and to other colonial posts.*

To John Holland Baker, later the Provincial chief surveyor, Butler owed the Erewhon journey itself, though (as we shall see) this expedition was but one of several which Butler undertook. Baker, who liked fast horses and port wine, is familiarly remembered by Johannes Andersen, once an assistant: "When sitting in his chair speaking to an officer, or thinking, he would draw maps on his head with a blue pencil; I suppose it titillated his head pleasantly! I suppose he didn't know it also ornamented him."[35]

There were others in Christchurch with whom Butler undoubtedly was on familiar terms: Dr. Barker, the physician-photographer; Crosbie Ward, the parodist-journalist-politician; William Reeves, of the *Lyttelton Times*; J. Colborne-Veel, whose humorous articles for the *Press* Butler thought well enough of to read to his English friends;

---

* Acland says of Broome: "He was not . . . a very practical sheep-farmer, dividing most of his time on the station between writing poetry, and pig-hunting. When pig-hunting he several times got so enthusiastic that he fired his ram-rod out of his rifle."—*The Early Canterbury Runs*, p. 224. Lady Barker's accounts of pig and wild-cattle hunts tend to bear out this judgment.

the Pauli family; George S. Sale (also of *The Press,* later to be professor of classics at the University of Otago); W. H. Wynn-Williams, his solicitor, in whose parlor he worked off the emotional stress of the race with Caton by playing Bach fugues for two hours.

Social life, for a transient bachelor of means, was already based upon the familiar English pattern of the club. Within a year after his arrival, Butler became a member of the Christchurch Club, possibly through acquaintance with Dr. Haast, who lived there for two years before his marriage in 1863. The Club, which still survives, was founded in 1856 to furnish a residence for squatters when they were in town. "Soon after its formation," says Wigram, "an unsuccessful attempt was made to vest the control entirely in the hands of country members."[36] When in 1858 an acre of ground was secured as a permanent site, members took shares of £50 each to build a substantial structure—somewhat over £3,000 worth—designed by Mountfort and Locke, who had also designed the Provincial Council Chambers. The first general meeting in the new quarters was on May 1, 1862. As a country member, Butler qualified as one of the "signs of the zodiac," local tradition declaring that though the Club was started by twelve squatters as a town residence, there were never more than two of them visible at once.[37] Sagittarius, Taurus, Scorpio—one of these designations would not have been inappropriate for a future satirist.

Another local tradition says that Butler wrote in the visitors' book "There is no Bible in this house." The story is given credence by the fact that the Club's suggestion book (as of January 18–21, 1861) carries this entry in the handwriting of Alexander Lean:

That a Bible be bought and kept in the library for the use of members.

ALEXANDER LEAN
S. BUTLER
C. H. BROWN[38]

The Club quickly became a provincial shadow of its London counterparts—a place for the exchange of opinion on all possible subjects by gentlemen possessed of at least some degree of leisure. In "A Night at the Club; or, Christchurch in 1963," evidently written shortly after the opening of the Ferrymead railway, there is much to suggest the ferment of opinion that Butler was encountering and helping to leaven. The pointed references to Darwinism suggest the debate conducted in *The Press* by Butler earlier in 1863, and the description of the steam-driven automata is redolent of "The Book of the Machines." The scene is the library of the Club; present are two speakers, Old Prosy and New Member, amidst "decanters, glasses, &c."

OLD PROSY: It is a wonderful thing, James, how much the mind sympathises with the body, and when the frail element is in good condition, with what a happy self-complacency the inhabitant glows. I believe that a nice observer of literature might tell the very hour of the day in which any particular page was written; and, from a close observation and collection of the sentiments, might sketch a fair diary of the regimen of the author, and say whether he dined alone on a solitary steak, or with an assemblage of wits, on all the delicacies of the season.

NEW MEMBER: There is something in that; and by reducing your theory to a science, much might be done for literature. The friendly critic might at once point out a fault and its remedy; sound port wine for despondent poets, and severe cathartics for satirists and cynics. Of course, our paternal Government would take it up. And think of the glorious spectacle to be presented by all Canterbury attending at the Office of the Board for the Regulation of the Public Digestion, to receive the bi-monthly pill that should ensure temper and argument to our writers, comprehension and submission to our readers! Why, we should get rid of the whole school of sensation novelists, not to mention the other ravings of mental dyspepsia. By-the-by, what is that pamphlet at your elbow?

OLD P.: Professor Geo. Logic's "Attempt to prove the Earth is an Animal." He considers earthquakes as symptoms of indigestion, brought on by imbibing too much atmospheric nutriment.

NEW M.: There is a review of it in the last *Anti-Creation Gazette*. For my part I rather incline to the theory of the Anti-Chaos Society that the Earth works on a pivot. Have you seen Lady Darwina Buckle's new novel, "The History of a Family?"

OLD P.: No; what is it?

NEW M.: The family is her own, and the history begins with the founder, a really delightful old baboon; there is an autobiographical sketch of his great grandson, which brought tears to my eyes. The heroic monkey had such clear views of the glorious destiny of his race and such entire devotion to it, that he actually used to bite a slice off his eldest son's tail every morning before breakfast to hasten its development.

OLD P.: Didn't Lady Darwina's brother come to grief in Africa lately?

NEW M.: Yes; he went out to civilise Gorilladom. He got them to acknowledge the relationship, but in learning Gorilla he forgot his English; and when they ceased to be afraid of his gun, they grew tired of him, so he got eaten one day.

OLD P.: You were talking of Geology. Here is a letter to the Superintendent, suggesting that if a sufficient portion of the Plains were sown with blue paper, carefully buried at a proper depth, the mineral formations might be brought to crop out in properly labelled parcels.

NEW M.: A capital idea. . . .

Well, we have had a pleasant chat, but how is it we have the library to ourselves?

OLD P.: All the Members have gone to dinner. Did you not know that to-day was the celebration of the Lyttelton and Christchurch junction? Here comes one of the absentees full of news.

THIRD MEMBER (*entering*): A splendid evening. Dinner capital! The steam band playing all the time, only it's a pity the leader makes such a row with his flageolet on account of his boiler being in his inside. Waiting perfect. As I came out I saw a steam waiter salute a steam housemaid with the greatest gallantry; and at the stable a self-acting groom put his comb between his teeth and gave me change for half-a-crown with perfect facility and accuracy. . . .[39]

The conversation concludes by their all rushing out to see "Jim Crow —the only man in Christchurch who is not a Government officer."

This dialogue, besides suggesting the kind of thought eventuating in *Erewhon*, serves as a barometer of public feeling at the time. Not only was the tunnel to Lyttelton soon to be completed, but other railways were being projected, in particular the Main Southern road to

84

Dunedin. A contract for the first thirty-six miles of this road was signed on May 29, 1865, for £201,000, of which one-fourth was to be paid in waste lands at £2 per acre. Some objected to the use of public lands as payment for public works; others (including Rolleston) opposed the plan as premature, but the railroad fever was not easily broken.[40] In *Alps and Sanctuaries*, speaking of S. Marie della Neve ("Ste. Mary of the Snow"), Butler remarks, "I suppose in another hundred years or so we shall have a S. Maria delle Ferrovie—a St. Mary of the Railways."[41] Some New Zealanders of the 1860's were already inclined to cry "Too fast!" but at the time Butler, still in the glow of his Darwinian optimism, was not among them. His conversation in Christchurch with Edward Chudleigh (March 19, 1864) is indicative:

Reached town early. Had a long talk with Butler on various subjects, I think he is gone as far as man can go now, he is an ultra-Darwinian, he thinks Darwin in 200 years hence will be looked upon as a most wonderful philosopher, and possibly a prophet, he does not believe the Bible to have been written by men under the influence of divine inspiration, but by *good men,* he thinks it a book, for all social and moral purposes, full of moral truths, and a book to be followed. I think he does believe in an almighty something, somewhere; he does not believe there is a colossal etherial being, that pervades all space and matter, whoes [*sic*] person would pass through the densest matter as unconscious of resistance as a feather in a vacuum, he thinks the time will come when man, a very different being to the present worm, will look back on us much in the same light as we look on the Silurian Epoch, the names of all the great men that influence the world will be forgotten but their influence will be handed down from age to age, modified and infinitely improved, just as we feel the influence of the first invention of the lever, wheel, and pulley. Give the World time, an infinite number of epochs, and according to its past and present system, like the coming tide each epoch will advance on each, but so slowly that it can barely be traced, man's body becoming finer to bear his finer mind, till man becomes not only an Angel but an Archangel.[42]

This contrasts sharply enough with another passage in *Alps and Sanc-*

tuaries where Butler, speculating upon change and rates of change, concludes that "the present is about the only comfortable time for a man to live in, that either has been or ever will be. The past was too slow, and the future will be much too fast."[43]

The opulent feasting at the railway opening was characteristic of one important form of New Zealand entertainment, but there were others. Among the easiest provided and most generally satisfying were dances, attended by town and country alike. An account of one of these, in 1853, is a little on the grim side, but honest and vivid. Once more it comes from Henry Sewell, who was spending a few days in Christchurch at the Golden Fleece Hotel (popularly known as the "Cold and Fleas" in deference to the German accent of the proprietor, Herr Gartner). Returning to the Golden Fleece about four o'clock on a blustery afternoon—a sou'wester had begun pelting in—the visitor found that a Mr. Longden, merchant and auctioneer, had scheduled a dance for the evening in his auction rooms, just opposite.

It was in truth a most dreary and unlovely night. Nevertheless about ½ past six came a bevy of damsels (rather fair ones too) all the way from the Ferry—the Miss Townsends with sundry attendant cavaliers. They had come in the dray, sheltered somehow or another, I don't know how, but looking very cold and cheerless. So we gave them up our warm berths by the fire, and they all seemed to think it capital fun. In came sundry other intending ball-goers—young Mr. Ward, Mr. Lee the affianced of Miss Paul &c., &c. and the Common room of the Golden Fleece became merry and crowded. In due time from the other side of the road came the sounds of Pianoforte and Violin, and in short, there was a Ball. How the people came and went—whether they swam or waded or in what costume they crossed the sloppy wet grass of the open land, or the equally wet and far more dirty quagmires of the so-called roads, is to me a mystery. But so it is.

Moreover, it went on all night. A Mr. LeCren, Longden's partner, had ridden in from his sheep station, some thirty-five miles, and "swum a river or two, somewhat at the risk of his life." The talk, as reported, struck Sewell in much the same way as it did Butler a few years later upon his first arrival:

It is amusing to mark the different kinds of pedantry in the world. Here it all runs upon Stations—Sheep runs—good and bad Country. "So and so has a splendid run." "Have you seen the country south of the Rakaia?" —or "Have you been up by Double Corner?" This, with the account of a "Shakedown at Caverhills," or a "Camping out on the banks of the Selwyn" is the staple talk. It is a wild odd life, quite new, and as long as the novelty lasts not without interest.[44]

Ten years, however, had brought enough changes for the circumstances to be less strenuous and the company more elegant when Butler was one of the dancers.

Special holidays were commemorated—none more lavishly, it is likely, than the one in celebration of the Royal Marriage of Edward, Prince of Wales, with Princess Alexandra of Denmark. This took place on Commemoration Day, July 9, 1863, in nor'wester weather not unlike that for the railway opening, though in July the temperature would not have been so high. Two commemoration oaks were planted (see the cut from the *Illustrated London News*, p. 88), having previously been carried through the streets in a procession which included such attractions as 150 Maoris from Kaiapoi, 50 butchers with a banner inscribed "Roast Beef of Old England," a threshing machine, a plow on a dray, millers and bakers "in a large and handsome wagon," school children with flags, the clergy, and innumerable dignitaries in carriages. "Among the attractive participants were the printers," says Andersen,

. . . who in addition to the traditional press which, fixed in a decorated wagon, was worked along the route, had got up an elaborate representation of Caxton, the first English printer, the dress and other details copied from an engraving. There was an attendant "devil," in tight-fitting black skin, with fiery eyes, white horns, wig, and a most portentous tail. The flags and banners were effective, and a description will serve as a reminder to the older and a model and incentive to the younger generation. There was a large crimson banner, "The Caxton Club"; a blue and gold banner inscribed "The First English Printer, William Caxton, A.D. 1474"; a green and gold banner, "We Printers share the Universal Joy"; three white silk banners,

Illustrated London News

Royal Marriage festivities at Christchurch, New Zealand

with the first page of the *Lyttelton Times*, the *Standard*, and the *Press*, printed in gold, borne by three apprentices; then various silk banners, with mottoes in gold letters, "Speed the Printing Offices"; "The United Press of Canterbury"; "Emulation not Rivalry"; "God Bless the Happy Pair"; "The Throne, the Press, the People"; "Types are the Seeds of Knowledge"; "Naught can crush a Free Press"; "Tyranny trembles at the Creaking of the Printing Press"; and others. A crimson banner "Excelsior," with three standard-bearers on horseback, clad in scarlet, closed the printers' part of the procession.[45]

Precisely what part, if any, Butler took in this display we do not know. Unquestionably by now a member of the "United Press of Canterbury" by the simple fact of being on the ground and not unwilling to keep his hand in with an occasional piece composed in "emulation not rivalry," he must have been concerned in some fashion or other with the arrangements.

Town life, thus, on a modest but comfortable and occasionally stimulating scale, not only was available to Butler but was used by him to social advantage. For the man of substance Christchurch could render pioneering life a good deal less confining than pioneering life generally is. Not only that: it could offer a high quality of intellectual companionship, and even—most important of all for Butler—an outlet for the occasional poem or prose sketch. It would be difficult to overestimate how much the opportunity of a connection with *The Press* must have meant, under the circumstances, to a young Cantabrigian with a taste for self-expression.

To begin with, New Zealand had offered him only financial challenge, or so he had supposed. In actuality he encountered there all that was needful to turn him onto the track of authorship he was soon to find and follow. When he sailed for "Home" in June of 1864 he was already "Erewhon Butler."

Part II: Trails into *Erewhon*

Once the days were clear
Like mountains in water,
The mountains were always there
And the mountain water;

And I was a fool leaving
Good land to moulder,
Leaving the fences sagging
And the old man older
To follow my wild thoughts
Away over the hill,
Where there is only the world
And the world's ill,
                    sings Harry.

DENIS GLOVER

THE PRESS

One of the cleaverest men in N.Z.
EDWARD CHUDLEIGH, DIARY

B utler was certainly not the only "cleaver" man in New Zealand, though, to borrow the term of his friend Moorhouse, he might sooner or later have come to rank among the "heaviest intellect of the Province." Heavy intellect, it is clear, could be found on a sheep run (not necessarily Mesopotamia, either), however much the pressure of business, both private and public, may have kept a good deal of native talent from exhibiting itself more than incidentally and sporadically. Taste, nonetheless, was present; the Squire of Mesopotamia moved in a highly literate circle.

Without the stimulus of such people, his fellow "new chums" in a colony that was barely under way, Butler must have done one of two things: go back to England at the earliest possible moment, or become a professional squatter and merge into the landscape. He did neither, though he was part way along toward squatterdom, and liking it well enough, when he decided he could retire with honor and a modest fortune. The baggage he took home with him included *Erewhon,* as yet unwritten but very much in the "World of the Unborn," supplicating softly for its birth. How he readied himself, unconsciously, for the accouchement of this great satire has been implicit in what has been seen thus far of his New Zealand career. Inquiry turns now toward the specific influences which came to bear on him and offered him a frame for his rapidly maturing thought. How, in more precise terms than those already evident, did New Zealand prepare him for the task of writing?

Erewhon is a book whose contents some readers might term confusing, others miscellaneous, still others organically complex. Unlike *The Way of All Flesh,* it contains few convincing characters; its emphasis lies almost solely on ideas. Nor is it structurally well integrated; it was contrived around odds and ends already at hand, some of which we will encounter in the present chapter. Encouragement to write it came from several friends, most notably Frederick Napier Broome (lately of "Broomielaw," Canterbury) and Elizabeth Mary Ann Savage, the "little lame lady" whose canny editorial advice and unfailing intellectual sympathy meant so much to Butler during the early years after his return to England. (He met Miss Savage in 1867; she died in 1885.)

Erewhon deals with an amorphous civilization which makes scant pretense of really hanging together. But the separate institutions within the loose satiric framework are quite something else: one by one they fall under a withering scrutiny which unmasks their pretentiousness and tags their shortcomings: home and school, Church and State, law, medicine, and Mrs. Grundy. Then there is "The Book of the Machines," the hot core of the work which concenters the entire assault upon the several varieties of rigidity and foolishness. The mechanistic view of life, Butler felt most passionately, was the one great unpardonable intellectual sin. Let man beware lest he prepare his own descent into bondage: upon a purely mechanistic (which is to say, in Butler's view, Darwinian) hypothesis, how indeed could he escape it?

Thus we are taken through a kaleidoscopic side show of ecclesiastical "Musical Banks," "Colleges of Unreason," topsy-turvy court trials, and suchlike diversions and distortions, with the guide at our elbow suggesting, "Well, why not? What's to prevent it, if you really believe in mechanism?" And if that is the way life is, all the more reason for thinking that men must surely have committed suicide into it from some celestial "World of the Unborn," to be hoodwinked by hypocritical professionalists, subjected to devastating self-deceptions, and mourned at death only by artificial tears. *Erewhon Revisited* offers, in Professor Hanky, a sample of the most doctrinaire and arrogant kind of professionalism at work. The indissoluble link between the two books, widely separated as they are in time of composition, is their common appeal to good sense, invariably the key signature of enduring satire.

Very likely *Erewhon* could not have been written if Butler had remained in New Zealand, though we cannot be sure. But neither could it have been written if he had not lived there as long as he did, and under the right conditions to produce it. However much a pioneering situation offers as raw material for romance or satire, as the case may be, it is unusual to find a writing laboratory—a publication outlet—close at hand. Butler was more fortunate than those of his compatriots who did their pioneering under less auspicious circumstances. New Zealand in general, and Canterbury in particular, was favorable to his destiny. *The Press* offered just enough stimulus to energize an urge for authorship of a kind not to be satisfied by writing letters to Langar rectory.

As the letters themselves suggest, ties with England were surprisingly close. Reading matter from "Home" arrived a few months late, but it did arrive, quite regularly, and there was time in which to read if not always true leisure in which to write. Kennaway stated matters accurately when he said, "I believe (so closely does the new world in these days of steam and telegraph tread upon the heels of the old), that these colonists . . . are, in their social signs and orderings, little more than three months behind ourselves, even though a couple of oceans do roll their waves between us."[1] When the colonists wrote and published for themselves, therefore, they produced something of a character not commonly encountered in isolated frontier newspapers; they were scholars, a fair number of them at any rate.

For the first ten years the *Lyttelton Times* had served the Province, its first number being published January 11, 1851—less than a month after the arrival of the first Pilgrim ships. Its principal editor, Crosbie Ward, was a young man of Butler's stamp, an able combination of wit and practical sense. James Edward Fitzgerald, one of the powers of the Province, owned the paper at the outset and remained in control as editor until his election as superintendent of the Province in 1853. Editorial policy professed to impartiality and declared the journal independent of both the Canterbury Association and the Government of New Zealand. The London *Times* (July 5, 1851) welcomed its namesake in a tone of paternal admiration:

> It is certainly not a matter of astonishment that the Canterbury settlers should settle upon an organ half an hour after they were fortunate enough to reach a distant home; but it is really worthy of remark and admiration that all the conditions of a highly influential journal should present itself [*sic*] in an instant to an antipodean contemporary on a desert coast, quite as readily as to the journalist in the centre of this ever busy city. It is difficult to glance at the first number of the "Lyttelton Times," now before us, and associate its existence with a community not a month old. So far from being ashamed at our namesake, we are positively proud of his acquaintance, and envious of his power. If the editor can create so much out of nothing, what would he make of such a breeding heap as this of London?[2]

So ready a disposition to credit the colonies with intelligence and enterprise has been somewhat less than universal among British intelligentsia.

By 1861 Christchurch was already outdistancing Lyttelton and there was room for another paper. Neither became a daily very soon, but there was enough news and advertising to warrant publication two or three times a week. Fitzgerald was likewise proprietor of the Christchurch *Press* when it began on May 25, 1861 (price, *6d. The Press* is still published, and the price is now *3d.*) Though the "heaviest intellect of the Province" started the paper as a mouthpiece by which to oppose Moorhouse's tunnel project, there were conditions naturally favorable to survival and growth. In less than a month after its founding, the *Press* was printing Thomas G. Read's letter telling of the discovery of gold in Otago; by September the rush was on.

Anxiety over the American Civil War and the possible involvement of England marks most of the first year, but by April of 1862 it was possible for a lead article to express relief that war with America seemed less likely. In the event of war, New Zealand might have found herself under attack, and in any event her lifeline to Britain would have been seriously threatened. For this and other reasons, the American Civil War was rather completely reported all the way along.

A sympathetic Maori policy was another hallmark of *The Press;* when the war on North Island began in earnest, the Maori side received full justice, together with fairly frequent articles on Maori customs and character. Such an article as "Traditions of the Middle Island [South Island]" in April, 1862, expresses regret that the settlers know so little about Maoris. The fact that Fitzgerald had once held a post in the antiquities department of the British Museum would help explain this interest, which, it should be added, was shared by other early figures in New Zealand, most notably Sir George Grey. Even so, the Maoris in significant numbers were remote, which is by no means to say they were ignored. After all, there were 150 of them from Kaiapoi in the Commemoration Day parade.

Local politics received quite extensive coverage, with an occasional satirical thrust, as in the "Debate Extraordinary in the Provincial Council of Canterbury" (December 14, 1861). Local crime, also, was reported in detail: interrogation of prisoners, arguments of counsel, speeches of judges. Festing Jones states that for *Erewhon* "Butler took the judge's summing up of the case against the young man with pulmonary consumption from a newspaper report of a trial of a man found guilty of, if I remember rightly, theft, with scarcely more alteration than the name of the offence."[3] While it is more likely that the source was an English newspaper, it should be noted that Butler formed the habit of reading such matter in a small paper that sometimes contained little enough exciting news.

The usual *Press* format was eight pages, with advertisements taking a fair share of even so limited a space. Most of the advertising, naturally enough, related to land and stock, though the Christchurch merchants and the shipping firms advertised too, and there were the inevitable legal notices. Book reviews or literary notices were not regularly provided (imported periodicals sufficing), but now and then there would appear a poem, a humorous article on local discomforts or makeshifts, or a piece of satire. The presence of satire in itself argues an intellectual audience, and such for the most part were the readers and patrons of the *Press*.

In general, it can be said that although certain contributions by Butler proved later to be of more than ordinary significance, they were by no means unparalleled; if a wider-than-local literary fame had been predicted for any local writer, Samuel Butler might well have been considered only after one or two others had been nominated.

Since Mesopotamia occupied Butler's time for the better part of two years, we do not find him immediately associated with the *Press*. His acquaintance with Fitzgerald, however, was made quite early; he reports in *A First Year* that when he bought his horse, "Doctor," he had a letter of introduction from Fitzgerald to Doctor's owner. ("I thought I could not do better than buy from a person of known character, seeing that my own ignorance is so very great upon the subject."[4]) Doctor, a bay with the brand "P. C." on the near shoulder, was warranted to be a good strong river-horse; his price was £55—"as horses are going . . . not . . . much out of the way."

By the end of 1862, after spring shearing, matters were in good shape at Mesopotamia and Butler was finding more leisure to read and write. He was pondering religious questions, engaging himself with speculation which emerged in his pamphlet on the Resurrection. Scientific thought was also much in his mind. As the result of encoun-

Rangitata River and Southern Alps

John Pascoe

Southern Alps Sheep Country: Manuka Point, Rakaia Valley

William Packe

Robert Booth, *Five Years in New Zealand*

Two drawings of Mesopotamia in the 1860's

Early photograph of Mesopotamia

One of the last views of Butler's hut—about 1926 (The masonry structure, right, was an addition)

Courtesy of Mrs. Moon, Ashburton, Canterbury

Interior of a Mesopotamia hut, 1860's (Drawing by William Packe)

Memorial plaque on the Butler hut site

Joseph Jones

John Pascoe

Wool dray in the Rakaia Valley

John Pascoe
Rakaia riverbed from Mein's Knob ("Erewhon" lies up one of the valleys to the left)

Whitcombe Pass—to "Erewhon" (Painting by Sir Julius von Haast)

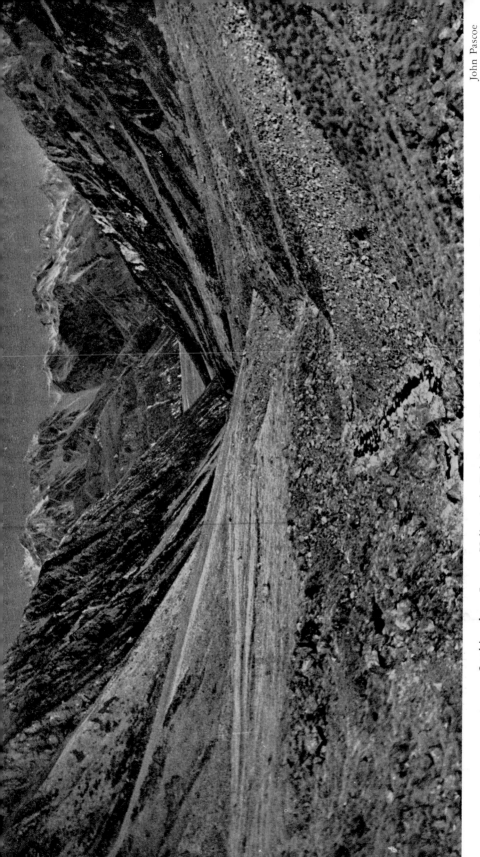

Looking down Louper Valley to the Rakaia (the "Erewhon" saddle is in the opposite range)

John Pascoe

"Maories disputing the right of territory"

Maori tiki at Raroera Pah (Drawing by George French Angas, 1847)

Christchurch Club, about 1864

Dr. A. C. Barker

Ferrymead Railway Terminal, 1863

Canterbury Museum

Samuel Butler: self-portrait in the McDougall Gallery, Christchurch

tering *On the Origin of Species* he entered the columns of *The Press* with what was to become a rather protracted exchange of letters, the chief portions (but not all) of which have been reprinted. The opening gambit, in the issue of December 20, 1862, was a dialogue between "F" and "C," the first of the two speakers posing as the warm advocate of Darwinism and the second a skeptic. F likes Darwin for his "judicial calmness"—a habit of mind "essential for any really valuable and scientific investigation." Upon C's flat statement that he simply does not like the book, F begins to "catechize" him to refute what he considers popular errors about Darwinism. He demonstrates by using local examples (e.g., cats on the large sheep-runs breeding rapidly and living on the fast-diminishing quail, thereupon competing among themselves for survival during famine). But despite F's exposition, C is still convinced that it is "very horrid" and "utterly subversive of Christianity." F is unwilling to admit any irreconcilable conflict between Darwinism and Christianity; he offers still another résumé of the Darwinian theory and closes by recommending that C read *On the Origin of Species* again. C replies that he does not intend to trouble himself further about the matter.

Shortly thereafter (January 17, 1863) came "Barrel-Organs," with the assertion that the Darwinian theory is merely an old tune being played again—"a *réchauffée* of the old story that his namesake, Dr. Darwin, served up in the end of the last century to Priestley and his admirers, and Lord Monboddo had cooked in the beginning of the same century." European ideas come from the Orient, new ideas from old; possibly Prometheus was the "first Darwin of antiquity." Though Darwinism is really not related to religious questions, it is erroneously supposed to be, and draws much of its interest from such motivation: if such were not the case, "no one would waste his time reading about the possibility of Polar bears swimming about and catching flies so long that they at last get the fins they wish for."

At this point it is pertinent to recall a statement Butler makes to Darwin in a letter dated October 1, 1865:

99

The first dialogue on the *Origin* which I wrote in *The Press* called forth a contemptuous rejoinder from (I believe) the Bishop of Wellington— (please do not mention the name, though I think that at this distance of space and time I might mention it to yourself)—I answered it with the enclosed, which may amuse you. I assumed another character because my dialogue was, in my hearing, very severely criticised by two or three whose opinion I thought worth having, and I deferred to their judgment in my next. I do not think I should do so now. I fear you will be shocked at an appeal to the periodicals mentioned in my letter, but they form a very staple article of bush diet, and we used to get a good deal of superficial knowledge out of them. I feared to go in too heavy on the side of the *Origin* because I thought that, having said my say as well as I could, I had better now take a less impassioned tone: but I was really exceedingly angry.[5]

Whether his critics were fellow members of the press, residents at the Club, or others, Butler does appear to have taken them seriously enough to disguise himself subsequently under the initials "A. M." In the first of a number of items headed simply "Darwin on Species," the supposed third party (A. M.) replies (February 21, 1863) that the author of the dialogue is a good earnest fellow, "and though his lights are not brilliant ones, yet he has apparently done his best to show the theory on which he is writing in its most favourable aspect." But for all this, he is "rash, evidently well satisfied with himself, very possibly mistaken, and just one of those persons who (without intending it) are more apt to mislead than to lead the few people that put their trust in them." The second writer, however, indulges in *non sequitur*'s to show why Darwin's theory is wrong, and is ungenerous in the construction placed upon passages alluded to. Both correspondents are extreme, A. M. thinks, and proceeds to point out that Darwinism is at least being seriously debated in the leading British magazines and before the British Association. This being so, it is "not to be set down by off-hand nicknames in Canterbury." [By and by the Darwinians, along with too many others, were to dismiss Butler with the "offhand nick-name" of "Erewhon Butler"—and he did not like it.] The naturalists themselves are the ones to decide; meanwhile, outsiders should not form hasty opinions for or against the theory, no matter what its plausibility may be. As to the fly-catching polar bear, Darwin must not be misrepresented as believing that the bear will or can develop into a whale; there is nothing in the text to indicate that Darwin thinks so, and to impute such "nonsense" to him is "disgraceful."

Next (on March 14) "The Savoyard" undertakes to supply from the *Botanic Garden* of Erasmus Darwin (Charles' grandfather) a passage which "contains the germ of Mr. Charles Darwin's theory of the origin of species by natural selection," quoting further extracts to illustrate the theory. Then A. M. replies (March 18) that the elder Darwin's speculation can hardly be offered as argument that Charles Darwin's theory is wrong; at best it is only "the crudest and most unshapen germ." Granting that most theories have speculative forerunners, with Darwin's no exception, the "clear and connected form" of the *Origin of Species* displays "the conclusion arrived at by a man of known scientific achievements after years of patient toil" and has merited the "full attention of the scientific world." [These sentiments, soon enough, must have had ironic—not to say embarrassing—overtones for Butler if he ever reread them, for within a few years he became an unremitting opponent of Darwin and Huxley.] A. M. does not wish either to attack or defend Darwin, but his "indignation was roused at seeing him misrepresented and treated disdainfully." He wishes "The Savoyard" would have "condescended to notice that little matter of the bear": he has searched his copy of Darwin and can see nothing but what was quoted in his previous letter.

Then comes (March 28) an article headed "Darwin and the Novelists,"* observing that though "no one accustomed to the processes of a

* This is one of four new items from *The Press,* either by Butler or associated with him, to be treated in this chapter:
  1) "Darwin and the Novelists," March 28, 1862 (Appendix A).
  2) Letter signed "Nimmer Beschweift," April 2, 1863 (Appendix B).
  3) "From Our Mad Correspondent," September 15, 1863 (Appendix C).
  4) Review of *A First Year in Canterbury Settlement,* October 28, 1863 (Appendix D).
The full text of each appears in the appendices as noted. A total of fourteen

rigid logic can accept Darwin's conclusions as proven," he has cleared the ground considerably—so thoroughly that "his worst enemies must consider him a writer of the greatest calibre." But there are still difficulties; man's possession of language, as Max Müller has intimated, "creates a vast and impassable chasm between man and all other created beings," and there is the additional fact that man is hardly the most powerful animal and therefore the best adapted to survive. Darwin must deal with these and other difficulties. But while Darwin has been busy scientifically, the imaginative writers have also begun to depict "the manner in which man may partake of the nature of the lower forms of animal life." Two recent American novels [Hawthorne's *Transformation* (English title of *The Marble Faun*) and Holmes's *Elsie Venner* (Holmes by some quirk is called Wendell Phillips!)] deal with the intermixture of animal and human nature. Hawthorne is particularly successful in suggesting that "if Darwin's theory be true, then the old Greeks were right:—it was through the phase of Fauns and Satyrs that man rose from the beasts of the field, and modern science after all but establishe[s] the fables of heathen mythology."* Impressed by "Darwin and the Novelists," a correspondent (April 2) signing himself Nimmer Beschweift ("Never-Tailed") wonders whether "Darwin's great theory" might not be adopted "without any inconsistency" as applying to all creatures *except* man. Since man is the only reasoning creature, the Darwinian theory

---

pieces in *The Press* over a little more than a year (December 20, 1862, to February 15, 1864) are attributable to Butler or otherwise connected with him. It seems doubtful that he wrote them all; on the other hand it seems probable that he wrote still other pieces that cannot be certainly identified as his, perhaps a good many such.

* Somewhat roundabout evidence that Butler may have been the reader of *Elsie Venner* and the writer of "Darwin and the Novelists" is adducible from *Erewhon*. Dr. Holmes was so much concerned with two matters—refuting the Calvinist dogma of original sin and developing his counterthesis of the essential identity of physical and mental disease—that *Elsie Venner* is somewhat less a novel than a tract. Thus we are prompted to wonder, confronted with "Darwin and the Novelists," whether Butler may not have imbibed some of his *Erewhon* notions about the reversibility of physical illness and moral lapse from reading *Elsie Venner* in New Zealand.

would be referred to man's mind instead of his body anyway; "it may be gravely doubted whether men were ever other than they are in form."

With the re-entry of "The Savoyard" (April 11) the "little matter of the bear" comes under discussion again, and the writer identifies himself as the writer of the "Barrel-Organs" letter. Darwin *did* say that he saw no difficulty in a race of bears "being rendered by natural selection more and more aquatic in their structure and habits, with larger and larger mouths, till a creature was produced as monstrous as a whale." Furthermore, this very passage suggests Buffon's theory of ascension, by which a bear "might pass into a seal, and that into a whale."

At this point the editor steps in to remark that the correspondents seem to be quarreling with each other because of differences in editions. A. M. is supported by "the only edition in our hands . . . the third, seventh thousand"; however, "we have heard that it is different in earlier editions, but have not been able to find one." It would appear that Darwin "was ashamed of the inconsequent inference suggested" and withdrew the passage.

A. M. (June 22) has one more word to say—or rather, to quote— from the *Saturday Review* of January, 1863. The records of the Zoological Society of London enumerate "three examples of hybrids between two perfectly distinct species," overthrowing "the commonly accepted theory that the mixed offspring of different species are infertile inter se." There must be other evidence, and at least there could be other researches made, "to make or mar that part of Mr. Darwin's well-known argument which rests on what is known of the phenomena of hybridism." With the fear that "both you and your readers will be dead sick of Darwin," he closes with his compliments to "The Savoyard."

It would hardly be worth reviewing all this colonial teapot-tempest (surely there must have been hundreds of similar exchanges over Darwin's ideas) were it not that the skirmishing finally led up to the essay called "Darwin Among the Machines," which gives us the first intimation of the *Erewhon* to come. And there are premonitions, likewise, for the years after *Erewhon* (which appeared in 1872). At this point, then, it may be useful to anticipate, a little, Butler's later writings on Darwinism in order to recognize their origins more clearly.

There are two sharply disparate eras in Butler's relations with Darwinism: first, the New Zealand years and a short period thereafter during which he champions Darwin as a liberator; then, disillusion, reversal of opinion, personal estrangement with Darwin, and finally a thirty years' war beginning in the later 1870's and ending only with death, in 1902. The campaigns of this war involve a series of books in which Butler both attacks Darwin and defends some of his predecessors. He studies and quotes various editions in an attempt to trap Darwin in modifications and presumptive falsifications; he invokes Buffon and Lamarck and Erasmus Darwin—men whose pioneer thinking, he feels, has been studiously neglected, not to say purloined; he proposes his own theories of habit and unconscious memory as something to substitute for the "mindless universe" implicit in materialism. The compulsion to continue such an unequal and unprofitable exchange was such (he came at last to believe, not without reason) as to thwart his career. How much of all this, we might well inquire, was Butler introduced to in New Zealand? Was he learning polemics along with pastoralism?

We have encountered, in the exchange just surveyed, a complex of attitudes toward Darwin. It does not seem quite reasonable to suppose that Butler wrote all the pieces; the "A. M." letters, however, may be assigned to him as one who is impressed by Darwin and wishes the Darwinian theory to be taken seriously. It is interesting that "The Savoyard" brings into the argument precisely the writers by whom Butler was later to set so much store: Buffon and Erasmus Darwin, though not Lamarck. There is, moreover, the revelation that different editions of *On the Origin of Species* did say different things—almost a prophecy of the meticulous comparisons of editions and phraseology by which Butler was to harass the Darwinians some years later. The seed of a suggestion that Darwin might have been "ashamed" of something, and suppressed it in later editions, has been planted. People could debate Darwinism in Christchurch as well as in London, and they did so; furthermore, they succeeded in beating down Butler's guard and calling into question his sudden enthusiasm. He was a sadder and wiser Darwinian, though still a militantly professing Darwinian, according to Chudleigh's report of 1864. But what might be the fruit of the doubt engendered by the introduction of names like Buffon and the other, the older Darwin? And what of the other correspondents who had taken up so vigorously for mind against mechanism? Whether he was aware of it or not, Butler already had been given his cue.

Whether (as Butler's letter to Darwin says) "The Savoyard" was the Bishop of Wellington, or somebody else, Butler had found an adversary who would stay with him in an argument—indeed, who would take the offensive against Darwin's supposed originality and drive Butler back to the rather ignominious position (he admits as much in his letter to Darwin) of asserting that anyone who had attracted as much attention at "Home" from the savants and the magazines ought to be treated with more respect in the colonies. Neither was it altogether generous (or accurate) of him to refer to his fellow colonists as "offhand nicknames in Canterbury" who had no business challenging the almighty Darwin. He was courting trouble by what might easily be looked on as egregiousness; moreover, in *A First Year in Canterbury Settlement*—a new-born lamb being dropped in England at almost the very moment he was retiring not too gracefully from the Darwinian controversy—he showed his adversaries a fair target.

Out of defeat came triumph, however, when, deserting argument, Butler let his mind romp over Darwinism in association with such evidences of progress as the new electric telegraph between Christchurch and Lyttelton, the Ferrymead railway and the tunnel—these, and better roads, and a Rakaia bridge, and all that the province as a sturdy pioneer infant was crying for. Almost as if half-convinced by his opposition, he

105

drops the cudgels and offers his readers an entre'act called "Darwin Among the Machines" (June 13). This, in summary, says:

> Though we are proud of improvements, we may well look upon the vast development of machinery and ask ourselves where we are going. We should be aware that an entirely new kingdom has recently sprung up which in time will be much more complex and extensive than now. Incapable of the task of classifying machines and dealing with them from the natural-historical point of view, we can at least point out the field as worth investigation.
>
> Machines have tended to get smaller as they progress: the cumbersome clock has become a small and beautiful watch. Daily developing the machines as we are, we may some day become the inferior race, looking up with awe at the serene and mighty machines, which will be fed, healed, and given new phases of existence. Thus, man will be inferior, but will be well-treated because of his necessity to the machines; at least he is necessary now, though he may not be so in the remote future. We are becoming daily more subservient; our complete subjugation is simply a question of time.
>
> The solution is war to the death: abolish machines before we are enslaved. For the present, we leave the matter in the hands of the Philosophical Society.

(The "Philosophical Society" would be the Canterbury Philosophical Institute, founded a year previously—July 24, 1862—by his friend Haast and others to study and care for such things as the moa bones that Butler and his neighbors were excavating.)

With this essay, it is no exaggeration to say, Butler had found—possibly had merely stumbled upon—the vein he was best suited to work. From that point forward he began digging the ore that in another decade would be smelted into *Erewhon.* Thus in June, 1863, in a colonial newspaper at the Antipodes, the conscious history of *Erewhon* begins.

A comparison of "Darwin Among the Machines" with "The Mechanical Creation" (published in London, in *The Reasoner,* on July 1, 1865) shows "The Book of the Machines" in process of evolution and reveals also a certain change of tone. "The Mechanical Creation" is not significantly longer but it is beginning to take the cast of closer and more compacted reasoning: there are six paragraphs, for example, as against an earlier nine; the Darwinian basis of the argument is developed at considerably greater length; and the cry for the abolition of machines is omitted. There is an impression that Butler is more seriously interested in the key idea, and yet one would say there is more life in the earlier piece—more illustrations, a more playful satiric spirit, a quicker tempo.

Following "Darwin Among the Machines" *The Press* published at length (September 15, almost exactly three months later) a sketch headed "From Our Mad Correspondent." This writer reports that he has taken the "Machines" letter altogether seriously (as the Erewhonians did their philosopher) and abolished all machinery of any kind about his household with the result that now he has no household left. He decides therefore to "go over to the enemy" and begins plotting, in league with the machines, for the "grand annihilation of time and place which we are all striving for, and which in one small part we have been permitted to see actually realised." (The Ferrymead railway was nearing completion.) Mind and body, Mad Correspondent goes on to say, are interrelated in such a way that the development of machinery must depend upon the development of the human mind and body as well. Means of communication are the key to "increased facility for the action of mind upon mind," as a survey of human records from the crudest attempts at message-making will show. With the Renaissance and Reformation,

Letters had done their work: they had fixed mind and bottled it, corked it, labelled it, laid it in bins, or libraries if you like it better, and so time was annihilated as regards the action of mind upon mind. Hence the progress. What the reformation did was this—it afforded few fresh facilities for the interchange of opinion—but it gave freedom to form opinion, freedom to utter opinion—and a secure home for freedom has, in consequence of the reformation, been at last founded in this British empire.

Interspersed with these somewhat rambling reflections are pleas for such practical things as a Rakaia bridge and a public library.*

Was Butler the "Mad Correspondent"? The grasp of—and interest in—the humorous implications of "Darwin Among the Machines" suggests his hand, as does also a reference to Handel's "Israel in Ægypt": "the back country squatter may hear his wool sold in London and deal with the buyer himself—may sit in his own chair in a back country hut and hear the performance of Israel in Ægypt at Exeter Hall—may taste an ice on the Rakaia, which he is paying for and receiving in the Italian opera house in Covent garden." An additional bit of evidence is supplied by an entry in the *Note-Books* ("Trail and Writing") which develops the idea that an intentional trail is "the first mode of writing," leading on to written symbols of all sorts which are the *sine qua non* of civilization. This, Mad Correspondent says also, and in the same terms. Finally, there is Butler's statement in *Unconscious Memory* that "a few days or weeks later than 13th June 1863 I published a second letter in the *Press* putting this view [that machines are extracorporeal limbs] forward."[6] His own copy of this letter, he goes on to say, was lost before *Erewhon* was written; but he would not likely describe as "a few days or weeks" the interval between "Darwin Among the Machines" (June 13, 1863) and "Lucubratio Ebria" (July 29, 1865)—the other piece on machines as extra limbs. Butler is most probably the author. But since others had already entered into the discussion of Darwinism, theoretically it might have been Butler *or* somebody else; there were others capable of doing such things and enough concerned to try.

By the time the "Mad Correspondent" letter appeared, Butler had reason to begin thinking himself a bit of an author, particularly with the knowledge that he had a whole book in press at "Home." *A First Year in Canterbury Settlement*—our source of most of the directly

* For the complete text, see Appendix C.

personal information about Butler's New Zealand experience—was published in London by Longmans in July, 1863. Butler's later view of this book is well known: he repudiated it in terms approaching savagery, numbering *Erewhon* as "Opus I" and aspersing *A First Year* at every opportunity. Why? Was it because his father had edited the material and arranged for the publication? Butler, to all appearances, came to think so, but at the time of its compilation there is no evidence of such an attitude. He wrote, in fact, somewhat jubilantly that he had "written a useful book, every word of which is true."[7] Un-Erewhonian as *A First Year* may be, there is not sufficient internal evidence to damn it as Butler did, especially since he had seen the manuscript and had had the opportunity of correcting it. G. D. H. Cole seems quite sound in his judgment that "the Canon's act in editing and publishing *A First Year in Canterbury Settlement,* based on his son's graphic letters home, was not that of a man who was set on putting the son down, or without appreciation of his qualities."[8] Moreover, the Canon was playing doubly safe by enlisting his son's consent and co-operation. One might speculate that Butler formed a dislike for *A First Year* because its compilation did not fit the pattern of the "World of the Unborn" 's insistence on being written, a pattern that characterized his other books: "They come to me and insist on being written, and on being such and such," and so on—the author-in-spite-of-himself of the *Note-Books.* But the speculation is unlikely; and anyway there was a degree of pressure, of necessity, that produced the letters home. At the same time, there was a conscious effort to be lucid and entertaining.

In London the *Athenaeum* received *A First Year* with some kindness, observing that though the author was not a practiced writer he had managed to deliver a good deal of useful information to prospective settlers. All this was calculated to please a young author; the circumstances point rather clearly toward the volume as a peace offering which Butler was not unready to accept. The chances are he felt rather good about it—up to a point.

The seed of discontent was sown, and perhaps the crop of rejection itself was harvested, in a review of *A First Year* which appeared at

Christchurch in *The Press* on October 28, 1863.* The reviewer said—
less in earnest, it would seem, than tongue-in-cheek—that if it was
really Samuel Butler who wrote this stuff, he should have had better
sense than to permit its publication; that it was tedious, egregious,
quite uncalled-for.

What are we to make of this? The impression of some well-
concealed horseplay about the piece is hard to shake off. Who produced
it we have no way of telling, but its effects on Butler may be estimated
with some accuracy. If—as is not impossible, certainly—the author was
Butler, then some severity on the part of those "whose opinion I
thought worth having" must have preceded and precipitated it. As
"A. M." in the Darwinian series, he had already reflected upon himself
as rash, self-satisfied, far from brilliant; and on the whole there is a
fair bit to incline one toward believing that Butler wrote the thing
himself.

On the other hand, it should be remembered that he had laid himself open to retaliation by a reference to "offhand nicknames in Canterbury" during the Darwinian exchange, and that *A First Year* is not
entirely free of sentiments that confirmed provincials might stick at:
it looks askance at the drinking habits of squatters; it dissertates a little
pompously on the relations of master and servant; it patronizes the
scenery. But whichever way it was, Butler was shortly in agreement
with everything derogatory that had been said; and it seems clear that
this *Press* review must be regarded as a principal feature in the background of his strange vindictiveness toward the book.

At this point of perplexity it may be of conjectural value, at least, to
introduce the enigmatic figure of Charles Paine Pauli, an Oxford man
whom Butler met at Christchurch through his associations with *The
Press,* where Pauli was employed as one of the editorial staff. Pauli
was to become for Butler, in later years, an incredible incubus. It was
both sympathy and admiration which first attracted Butler to the
younger man (Butler was twenty-eight, Pauli about twenty-five at the
time of their first association). Ill with a mouth-and-throat infection,

* For the text, see Appendix D.

Pauli had convinced himself that a continuing residence in New Zealand must mean early death. Butler believed so, too, and offered to pay his way back to England, arrange treatment for him, and supply him funds until he could get on his feet again. The two traveled together on the way home, and Pauli lived for a time at Clifford's Inn, where Butler took rooms. Butler's assistance Pauli accepted—and for more than thirty years continued to accept, subtly managing to extract, either through blandishment or tacit extortion, a substantial regular allowance through bad fortune and good until he died in 1897. So coolly did he manage affairs that he kept his patrons, of whom he had several, at such a distance from himself and from each other that none knew the truth until the time of the funeral. Thus was the great ironist himself ironized—with a vengeance. Suspicion easily weaves dark webs around so curious an association, but the only facts we have are noncommittal. It is evident enough, however, that Pauli, who by all available testimony was the kind of sociable, well-spoken, easy-appearing "nice person" that Butler felt himself never quite able to become, was a most calamitous hostage to his benefactor's fortunes. In vain had Moorhouse counseled Butler that "very handsome, well-dressed men are seldom very good men."[9]

What, if anything, Pauli had to do with concocting the *Press* review is likewise matter for speculation only, but interesting enough speculation. Did Pauli, who entered Butler's life about this same time, offer him sympathy, or flattery, or some other variety of counterfeit understanding? And how is he to be associated with Butler's later antipathy to his book? Butler thought of *A First Year,* or was soon persuaded to think of it, as a mortgage upon any future fame. A shrewd blackmailer would not be likely to overlook so useful a bit of potential pressure on a proud spirit, and unquestionably Pauli knew all about it.

Any close association between Pauli and the book, or the review, must be extrapolated from the sketchy amount we know of him. We do know, however, that Butler thought highly of Pauli's literary judgment —too highly, in all likelihood—and that Pauli was his legal confidant in matters relating to Canon Butler. It takes no very far-fetched conjecture to suppose that Pauli saw his own interest being well served in a continuing estrangement, and we might well wonder whether Butler was astutely inveigled into his low opinion of *A First Year* and thence to further animosity against those responsible (along with himself) for what he came to regard as the blunder of its publication. Something operated quickly and powerfully to induce a lifelong hostility toward his innocent little first-born book. Whatever it was is closely bound up with the *Press* review; and of Pauli one may be not unjustly suspicious. Pauli worked his cards very adroitly, and this review would have fitted neatly into the pack.

A few weeks later, at the railway celebration, Butler's public denial of "all connection with the Press of Canterbury or with Mr. Samuel Butler of the Rangitata district" comes as an echo of the review. But whatever the motives or consequences may have been, Butler continued his association with *The Press* and, not long before leaving, contributed a sportive piece of verse occasioned by the visit of a cricket team: "The English Cricketers." Many lines merely echo the Tennysonian belief in "progress"—already a colonial cliché. In some, however, we sense "Mad Correspondent's" concern with the annihilation of space:

> .   .   .   .   .   Mark me well,
> Matter as swift as swiftest thought shall fly,
> And space itself be nowhere   .   .   .
> Mirrors shall hang suspended in the air,
> Fixed by a chain between two chosen stars,
> And every eye shall be a telescope
> To read the passing shadows from the world.

"Horatio," who sees this vision, admits that he is drunk (the same expedient is used later in "Lucubratio Ebria"); but that it was Butler's mood at the time, shared by his fellow colonists, seems evident from his conversation with Chudleigh.

"Lucubratio Ebria," the last of Butler's known contributions to *The Press,* appeared about a year (July 29, 1865) after his departure. A complement to "Darwin Among the Machines," it sees machines not as a threat but as supplementary limbs: "the mode of development by which human organism is most especially advancing." This of course became the counterargument to the mechanophobia of *Erewhon.* Such ideas had been advanced already by Mad Correspondent, who promised to follow his letter of September 15, 1863, with others. More than likely "Lucubratio Ebria" is part of a projected series which Butler's return to England interrupted and (after what was already drafted had been disposed of) terminated.

Whether from nostalgia or to meet the demands of a complicated plot, Butler uses in *Erewhon Revisited* a newspaper story, a "veracious extract" from the "Sunch'ston bi-weekly," offering a short-circuited version of events and at the same time a rather unveracious "official" account of Higgs's second visit to Erewhon. If Butler was thus recalling his days of reading *The Press* and writing for it, he had not forgotten the old tricks. The "Sunch'ston bi-weekly" parallels, satirically, the *Press,* the *Lyttelton Times,* and other colonial sheets.

In all, the importance of *The Press* to Butler's literary career was considerable. It gave the potential author in him an outlet when he needed it and let him undergo, as Fort says, "trial by print." In a span of slightly more than two years he moved out of polemics into light satire. The public he faced, moreover, was highly intelligent and critical—more intensely so than any he was to reach in England after *Erewhon.* "Providence, as luck would have it," also threw Pauli in his way, but Pauli was only the representative of a very capable group. As one of the *Press* coterie, Butler proved himself capable of standing up to a vigorous marshaling of ideas even as he had stood up to the mustering of recalcitrant sheep. From his opponents he was receiving the outlines of the attack he was himself to make upon the fundamental positions of Darwinism. He was being intellectually groomed for *Erewhon;* and if, according to his theory of unconscious memory, the things which are done best are done most nearly automatically, he had already begun the automatic process of producing a major satire. Most of us would suppose, however, that there must have been at least a little deliberation.

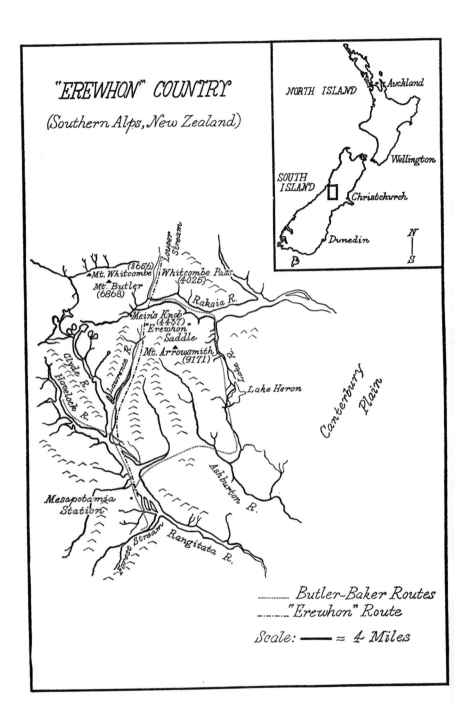

"EREWHON" COUNTRY

(Southern Alps, New Zealand)

NORTH ISLAND

Auckland

Wellington

SOUTH ISLAND

Christchurch

Dunedin

N
W   E
S

(8656)
▲ Mt. Whitcombe
Mt. Butler
(6868)

Louper Stream

Whitcombe Pass
(4025)

Rakaia R.

Mein's Knob
(4437)
"Erewhon"
Saddle

Mt. Arrowsmith
(9171)

Clyde R.
Havelock R.

Laurence R.

Lake R.

Lake Heron

Canterbury Plain

Ashburton R.

Mesopotamia
Station

Forest Stream

Rangitata R.

.... Butler-Baker Routes
_._._._ "Erewhon" Route

Scale: ——— ≈ 4 Miles

EREWHON: GEOGRAPHY

*Exploring is delightful to look forward to and
back upon, but it is not comfortable at the time,
unless it be of such an easy nature as not to deserve
the name.*

EREWHON

The words of *Erewhon* were written in England, but much of its
substance was conceived and lived-out in New Zealand, which
already in Butler's time, as we have been observing, was ambitious of
becoming a microcosm of "Home." Moreover, it was fast succeeding
in doing so, most particularly in such places as Christchurch. A moderate primitivist of moderate means already had the choice of lodging in
the wilderness only so long as it pleased his fancy: he could live in the
Christchurch Club and retreat to the Southern Alps, or live in the
Southern Alps and retreat to the Christchurch Club, as Butler did. And
although the colonial microcosm offered only the rudiments or remnants of overblown institutions which a satirist might long to attack—
home, church, school, the professions, all with their vulnerable creeds
and incongruous hypocrisies—the ideological linkages with the base of
supply abroad were only too apparent.

Still, one feels, the full tide of British conventionalism must have
been setting against the author of this intriguing book. In the chapter

on the Colleges of Unreason, Oxford and Cambridge seem near enough to lob shells into; when one reads of the Musical Banks, he visualizes church edifices in already populous and overcozy cities; so too with the law courts and palaces and other interiors of Erewhon, in which various large segments of Victorian society are turned upside down for ironic scrutiny. *Erewhon* is at best a structurally miscellaneous book, as satires frequently are. Parts of it, even, were added many years after its publication and instantaneous success in 1872, for example, the diverting chapters "The Rights of Animals" and "The Rights of Vegetables." The reader wanders through its exhibits as through the booths at some fantastic fair. Not so, however, with the descriptive prelude recounting the explorations leading to the discovery of Erewhon: here is narrative of quite a different body and movement—the tough base of reality from which the arch to fantasy is sprung. To this prelude, and to some companion passages in *Erewhon Revisited,* we may turn with confidence to learn the meanings, for Butler, of the mountains at Mesopotamia and beyond. He leaned heavily upon his memory for such descriptions, upon his imagination almost not at all. It was, as H. J. Massingham says, an experience "unique in the annals of Englishmen whose books have raised them to the stature of immortals," for there is no "genuine literary analogy between the Butlerian interregnum among the Southern Alps of New Zealand and the withdrawals of poet or sage or critic of society from the vortex of human affairs into the solitudes of permanent Nature."[1]

The first five chapters of *Erewhon,* together with a few relevant additions from *Erewhon Revisited,* still form a most satisfying verbal introduction to the scenery of New Zealand. Far from being in guidebook style, they are nevertheless a kind of guidebook, for they are the epitome of Butler's exploring experience, which in turn is representative of the life lived by the early type of outdoor New Zealander. To a limited extent, that way of life still survives—or perhaps it would be better to say that the conditions under which it was lived are, in places, still near enough the same to afford a glimpse of what it used to be like; for though a few deer-stalkers and prospectors may still boil their tin "billies" for tea and sleep in their swags, most New Zealanders (except on holiday) are civilized and comfortable, if a little apologetic for being so.

But the bush is near, and it is the disposition of the people to want it near. They have preserved areas of native growth in or near towns and are tightly controlling what forests now remain after time's worst century of depredation. It would seem, on first thought, that an overwhelmingly pastoral economy would tend to preserve native conditions, but something nearer the opposite is true: grassland has replaced forest and bush, and the well-managed sheep run (except in the sparser high country) is quite an artificial phenomenon. Yet the bush is near, and even the casual visitor can stroll into the hills to encounter its mazes, curiously jungle-like for a temperate climate. . . . *Where'er you walk, cool gales shall fan the glade.* . . . Great trees press up through a thick cover of brush, vines, moss, and fern; ferns, some of them, grow into trees, suggesting an anachronistic remnant of the Carboniferous; and certain animal forms survive here that in other parts of the world are to be seen only in fossils. . . . *Trees where you sit shall crowd into a shade.* . . . It is not difficult to get lost; search parties are called out with some frequency, though not so often as in Australia, where the bush is a sort of green terror and where aborigines are employed like bloodhounds to track lost people. This kind of bush is more typical of upper North Island and the rain forests on the western slopes of South Island. Canterbury had (and still has) spots of it, but the plains and higher mountains are by comparison rather sparsely vegetated. Once the thicket is removed, the soil will support a perpetual cover for grazing. The settlers burned scrub, not usually whole forests, to provide grasslands for their flocks.

Level country is the exception, mountain scenery typical. Abel Tasman, the first European to see New Zealand, sighted the western mountains of South Island late in 1642 and wrote in his log, "Towards noon saw a large land, uplifted high." Dutch patriotism named this "land uplifted high," ironically enough, after a province of the flattest country in the world; poetry invaded geography much later to do ultimate justice to the "Southern Alps," which are rugged in the extreme. Partly because they were so formidable, partly because they promised so little of an immediate practical character, the Southern Alps had been made known only in the most cursory way when Butler came to Mesopotamia. Contemporary maps listed large sections of western Canterbury as "mountainous country unexplored."

For the explorer the river courses were the natural route. For man and beast it was necessary to stay somewhere near water; and although the shingle riverbeds were not the easiest footing, the rivers led most readily to the great central chain of mountains and to what one hoped would be negotiable passes. A few random sentences from the earlier part of *Erewhon* describe the standard procedure of exploration:

The first day we had an easy time, following up the great flats by the river side, which had already been twice burned, so that there was no dense undergrowth to check us, though the ground was often rough, and we had to go a good deal upon the river-bed. . . . The gorge was narrow and precipitous; the river was now only a few yards wide, and roared and thundered against rocks of many tons in weight; the sound was deafening, for there was a great volume of water. We were two hours in making less than a mile, and that with danger, sometimes in the river and sometimes on the rock. . . . Farther progress up the main river was impossible, for the cliffs descended like walls; so we went up the side stream, Chowbok seeming to think that here must be the pass of which reports existed among his people. . . . We followed every stream but one, and always found it lead us to a glacier which was plainly impassable, at any rate without a larger party and ropes. One stream remained.

One stream remained: this was to lead Higgs into Erewhon after Chowbok had legged it off in panic over what he knew would be found at the pass.

The pass to Erewhon is the Whitcombe Pass (elevation 5,025), a few miles north of the Rakaia River up Louper Stream, which flows into the Rakaia. Butler, with John Holland Baker, discovered this pass early in 1861. There are impressive mountains in the area: Mt. Whitcombe (8,656) and Mt. Evans (8,580) to the west and north, and—

not to be overlooked—Mt. Butler (6,868—part of the Butler Range) directly west of Louper Stream. Mt. Cook (12,349), the highest peak in New Zealand, lies fifty airline miles to the southwest. Everything between and on both sides is in the rugged heart of the Southern Alps.

But nothing resembling Erewhon, in actuality, lies on the other side; Whitcombe Pass leads into further desolation and is not as suitable for traffic as two passes farther north, both of them easier and lower (Arthur Pass at 3,038 and Lewis Pass at 2,386). It was gold fever in the 1860's that spurred the search for practicable overland transit to the West Coast, and to this epidemic Butler was not altogether immune, as both *A First Year* and *Erewhon* make clear. The name Whitcombe was given the pass (and to the neighboring mountain) in memory of Henry Whitcombe, drowned in the Taramakau, a West Coast river, while on a two-man expedition across the mountains, undertaken as a result of Butler and Baker's report of the pass. Whitcombe's companion, Louper (actually Lauper—Jacob Lauper, a trained Swiss mountaineer), managed to get back under short rations and no little hardship. It is for him that Louper Stream, abounding in waterfalls and "Blue Pools" of glacial water, is named. Of the upper Rakaia country Louper wrote:

High mountains rise up on both sides of the valley, with their tops covered with snow; further towards the south we could see glaciers, with perpetual snow, and it was in this direction that we must seek for a pass leading down to the West Coast across the mountains. I was sent on in advance to find a good camping ground. I walked fast, my thoughts recurring back to my native land. These mountains and glaciers reminded me of my young days, when oftentimes, light-hearted and free from care, I had wandered about in just such places. How things are changed since then![2]

Butler, like Louper, felt the loneliness. Much of the mountain country, he thought, lacked appeal because of the absence of human associations; unlike the European Alps, the Southern Alps are neither verdurous nor otherwise congenial to habitation by man. "Too savage," said Butler. The area is isolated to begin with, and the predominating gray of the rockslides and riverbeds combines with the tawny grasses to give an impression of desolation relieved only by the intense blue of the sky. On the eastern slopes there is very little bush in many places; one journeys across shingle, up valleys, over saddles, and into the central snow-clad range with the feeling of being on his way to Nowhere, unreversed.

Making his way home to Mesopotamia from the Ashburton gorge, Butler described the scenery in these terms:

There is no timber in this valley, and accordingly the scenery, though on a large scale, is neither impressive nor pleasing; the mountains are large swelling hummocks, grassed up to the summit, and though steeply declivitous, entirely destitute of precipice. Truly it is rather a dismal place on a dark day, and somewhat like the world's end which the young prince travelled to in the story of "Cherry, or the Frog Bride." . . .

Snow-grass, tussock grass, spaniard, rushes, swamps, lagoons, terraces, meaningless rises and indentations of the ground, and two great brown grassy mountains on either side, are the principal and uninteresting objects in the valley through which we were riding. I despair of giving you an impression of the real thing. It is so hard for an Englishman to divest himself, not only of hedges and ditches, and cuttings and bridges, but of all signs of human existence whatsoever, that unless you were to travel in similar country yourself you would never understand it.

After about ten miles we turned a corner and looked down upon the upper valley of the Rangitata—very grand, very gloomy, and very desolate. The river-bed, about a mile and a half broad, was now carrying a very large amount of water to the sea.[3]

On the other hand, he felt occasionally the power of the mountains in full measure:

The scenery soon became most glorious, for, turning around a corner of the river, we saw a very fine mountain right in front of us. I could at once see that there was a *névé* near the top of it, and was all excitement. We were very anxious to know if this was the backbone range of the island, and were hopeful that if it was we might find some pass to the other side. The ranges on either hand were, as I said before, covered with bush, and these, with the rugged Alps in front of us, made a magnificent view. We went on, and soon there came out a much grander mountain—a glorious glaciered fellow—and then came more, and the mountains closed in, and the river dwindled and began leaping from stone to stone, and we were shortly in scenery of the true Alpine nature—very very grand.[4]

Mt. Cook affected him similarly:

Suddenly, as my eyes got on a level with the top, so that I could see over, I was struck almost breathless by the wonderful mountain that burst on my sight. The effect was startling. It rose towering in a massy parallelogram, disclosed from top to bottom in the cloudless sky, far above all the others. It was exactly opposite to me, and about the nearest in the whole range. So you may imagine that it was indeed a splendid spectacle. It has been calculated by the Admiralty people at 13,200 feet, but Mr. Haast, a gentleman of high scientific attainments in the employ of Government as geological surveyor, says that it is considerably higher. For my part, I can well believe it. Mont Blanc himself is not so grand in shape, and does not look so imposing. Indeed, I am not sure that Mount Cook is not the finest in outline of all the snow mountains that I have ever seen. It is not visible from many places on the eastern side of the island, and the front ranges are so lofty that they hide it. It can be seen from the top of Banks Peninsula, and for a few hundred yards somewhere near Timaru, and over a good deal of the Mackenzie country, but nowhere else on the eastern side of this settlement, unless from a great height. It is, however, well worth any amount of climbing to see. No one can mistake it. If a person says he *thinks* he has seen Mount Cook, you may be quite sure that he has not seen it. The moment it comes into sight the exclamation is, "That is Mount Cook!—not, "That *must* be Mount Cook!" There is no possibility of mistake.[5]

The mountaineer in him led to the observation that "he who first scales it will be crowned with undying laurels: for my part, though it is hazardous to say this of any mountain, I do not think that any human being will ever reach its top." Butler lived, however, to see his prediction fail.

"Butler," writes John Pascoe, "will never be forgotten in the back country of Canterbury. His work is an inspiration to the present generation of mountain travellers."[6] And when Pascoe says "work," he means Butler's actual mountaineering, not just what is to be imagined from *Erewhon*. No better tribute might be asked, for Pascoe is one of Butler's breed of mountaineers. He has often stood where few or none have stood before, and to make his feats still more significant he has invariably had his camera with him. New Zealand, it will not be soon forgotten, trained men for Everest, and one of them got to the top.

The mountaineers and geographers of New Zealand have done well by Butler, on the whole, in commemorating him throughout the high country. There is a Butler Range (including Mt. Butler), a Butler's Saddle, an Erewhon Col and a Chowbok Col, and an Erewhon branch of the Canterbury Mountaineering Club (at Ashburton). Some of the names, moreover, might have been bestowed if *Erewhon* had not been written, for Butler earned for himself a creditable reputation as explorer.

Before coming to New Zealand he already had been attracted to mountains. One of his earliest pieces describes a journey to the Italian Alps in 1857—a three weeks' walking tour on a bedrock budget, during which Butler and his companion "Giuseppi Verdi" (Joe Green) walked forty-two miles in one long day. He had been to the Alps before and was to return several times, finally paying tribute to the region in *Alps and Sanctuaries,* a guileless and uncommonly warm-hearted book. The early pages of *A First Year* show him as a connoisseur of mountains, and it is easy to understand why the back country had no terrors for him: his New Zealand years only reinforced what was already on its way to becoming a lifelong passion. *Erewhon* levies upon a fund of expert and firsthand knowledge for its convincing detail.

Erewhon—the real Erewhon of the Southern Alps—is not often revisited. A few words from *Erewhon Revisited* will help explain why:

Another reason that made it more easy for Erewhon to remain unknown, was the fact that the more mountainous districts, though repeatedly prospected for gold, had been pronounced non-auriferous, and as there was no sheep or cattle country, save a few river-bed flats above the upper gorges of the rivers, and no game to tempt the sportsman, there was nothing to induce people to penetrate into the fastnesses of the great snowy range.[7]

Butler's geologist friend Haast had "pronounced non-auriferous" a good deal of the territory, and the proved impossibility of finding new grazing land made subsequent exploration seem pointless to all but the topographer or mountaineer—neither one so very numerous in New Zealand, at least for the serious "work." Mention of Haast recalls still another sort of exploration that Butler indulged himself in: paleontology, especially as related to the moa. Haast, an extraordinarily enthusiastic naturalist, must have had much to do with interesting Butler in prehistoric bones. Chudleigh recalls finding moa remains in the mountains and bringing back a number of leg bones, including "one for Butler." When the returning Higgs of *Erewhon Revisited* requires a plausible explanation for being in the high country, he tells a shepherd that he has "come to see if he can find traces of a large wingless bird, whose existence had been reported as having been discovered among the extreme head waters of the river."[8]

Since the supposed Erewhon journey is only one of several, it may be well to consider the full extent of Butler's activity in the mountains. By no means were all of his peregrinations pleasure trips. However congenial mountaineering may have been as a diversion, Butler was of necessity obliged to go searching for unclaimed land. As desirable sheep runs became scarcer, exploration became a regular part of the business for an entrepreneur, and Butler found himself thrust into the role of range-rider and mountaineer, whether he liked it or not. Fortunately, he did; he was flexible enough not to be daunted by frontier exigencies. All this is concentrated for us in the opening chapters of *Erewhon*. The young cadet responds to a combination of economic pressure from the coastal plains and a lure from the unknown interior; he makes his way up the river valleys and up to a pass where he finds a number of fantastic statues. Beyond lies Erewhon.

Most of Butler's exploring was done between the time of his arrival

123

in January, 1860, and September of the same year, at which time he established Mesopotamia Station. The Erewhon journey (January–February, 1861), which is of principal concern here, is plotted in some detail by Butler himself in a note written in 1884:

Up as far as the top of the pass, where the statues are, keeps to the actual geography of the Upper Rangitata district, except that I have doubled the gorge. There was no gorge up above my place and I wanted one, so I took the gorge some ten or a dozen miles lower down and repeated it, and then came upon my own country again, but made it bare of grass and useless instead of (as it actually was) excellent country. Baker and I went up the last saddle we tried, and thought it was a pass to the West Coast, but found it looked down on to the headwaters of the Rakaia; however, we saw a true pass opposite, just as I have described in *Erewhon,* only that there were no clouds and we never went straight down as I said I did, but took two days going round by Lake Heron. And there is no lake at the top of the true pass. This is the pass over which, in consequence of our report, Whitcombe was sent and got drowned on the other side. We went up to the top of the pass, but found it too rough to go down without more help than we had; I rather think I have told this in my N.Z. book, but am so much ashamed of that book that I dare not look to see. I don't mean to say that the later books are much better; still they are better.[9]

The station from which Higgs and Chowbok start out is evidently Mesopotamia for the most part, with more or less general similarity to other stations of the region:

How often have I sat on the mountain side and watched the waving downs, with the two white specks of huts in the distance, and the little square of garden behind them; the paddock with a patch of bright green oats above the huts, and the yards and wool-sheds down on the flat below; all seen as through the wrong end of a telescope, so clear and brilliant was the air, or as upon a colossal model or map spread out beneath me. Beyond the downs was a plain, going down to a river of great size, on the farther side of which there were other high mountains, with the winter's snow still not quite melted; up the river, which ran winding in many streams over a bed some two miles broad, I looked upon the second great chain, and could see a narrow gorge where the river retired and was lost. I knew that there was a range still farther back; but except from one place near the very top of my own mountain, no part of it was visible: from this point, however, I saw, whenever there were no clouds, a single snow-clad peak, many miles away, and I should think about as high as any mountain in the world.[10]

The mountain is, of course, Mt. Cook; the narrow gorge was borrowed from Forest Creek and made to fit the Upper Rangitata, but the description of the river itself is literal enough. Higgs as shepherd was assigned to what is called the "top beat":

It was my daily business to go up to the top of a certain high mountain, and down one of the spurs on to the flat, in order to make sure that no sheep had crossed their boundaries. . . . I had a telescope and a dog, and would take bread and meat and tobacco with me. Starting with early dawn, it would be night before I would complete my round; for the mountain over which I had to go was very high. In winter it was covered with snow, and the sheep needed no watching from above.[11]

The range above Mesopotamia, as already mentioned, affords such a view of Mt. Cook; *A First Year* records Butler's response to the grandeur of the peak as seen from this point, some thirty to thirty-five miles away. Edward Chudleigh describes the view in these terms:

I saw some most beautiful and grand seanery. I was on a hill about 1,500 ft. above the Rangitata, the snow-topped hills rise 8 and 9 thousand feet on my right and left, then lovely valleys covered with bush that you can follow up till they die away in the blue of the distant mountains whoes tips shoot up into a sky of spotless blew, at my feet there is fine undulating country spotted with small lakes or lagoons, and then come the Rangitata plains. The river loses its dreariness in distance and looks fit for any picture, here downs come in again, which very gradually rise into endless snow. I cannot describe the grandeur of this place. I wish I could paint it.[12]

When the "top beat" cadet-shepherd, therefore, falls to "speculating upon what might lie farther up the river and behind the second range," he is Samuel Butler wondering what is on up the Rangitata: more sheep country, he hopes (as does the young cadet), or possibly alluvial gold. Three upper forks converge to form the Rangitata: the Havelock, the Clyde, and the Lawrence, all named (by Dr. Haast) for military heroes in the Indian Mutiny of 1857. Nestling somewhere in the upper reaches of any one of the three, Butler permitted himself the luxury of imagining, might be found a tidy patch of a few thousand acres accessible to stock and otherwise suitable for a run. At least it would be sport to find out. And there was another young man who was undoubtedly just as eager as Butler.

In John Holland Baker, not yet quite twenty-one when the exploring trip took place, Butler had chosen a most useful companion. Baker, also a country clergyman's son, and nephew to Archdeacon Mathias, had arrived in the colony in May, 1857, and gone immediately to work as an apprentice surveyor. Early in 1860, in the company of his cousin Frank Mathias, he explored up the Waimakariri River and located a new sheep run of some 15,000 acres, the lease to which before long he had sold for £300. Later the same year he completed his three years of apprenticeship and, having met Butler in Christchurch, was invited to join him in another land-search. Accordingly, late in December of 1860 he reached Mesopotamia in time for Christmas dinner (the three who sat down at the table, he recalls, were a Butler, a Baker, and a Cook—Cook being shepherd-manager of the station).

It was their intention to see what lay on up the valley, or valleys, of the Rangitata, and on December 29 they set out to work their way up the Havelock branch. Only a few days' exploring was needed to convince them that no accessible "country" would be found in that direction. Both received a ducking on the way back to their camp; Baker writes that Butler

. . . was not more than a third of the way over when he was swept off his legs and was washed down the rapid. It was so funny to see his head and then his feet uppermost that I could not help laughing, and when he was through the rapid and I put out my pole to help him to land he was so indignant that he would not take it. . . . I don't think that the idea of being drowned crossed either his mind or mine.[13]

On New Year's Day they returned to Mesopotamia for a week's recuperation.

On the second penetration they followed up the Clyde far enough to satisfy themselves that there was no pass at the head and then went on up the Lawrence, the branch farthest to the north and east. Caught in a heavy downpour, they improvised a shelter among the rocks and spent the following day attempting to keep dry, during which interval "Butler told me yarns of his college days, his quarrels with his father, his studies as lay assistant at St. James in Piccadilly, and his final determination to come out to the colony."[14] Leaving their horses they climbed to the top of the ridge above the Lawrence (to a point somewhere near Mein's Knob) whence they looked down upon the riverbed of the Rakaia: a splendid view, but of territory already known. Looking across the Rakaia, however, they could see a low pass "evidently leading to the West Coast" but not practicably accessible from the direction they had come. Resolving upon still a third approach, they started back:

We were soon descending the snow slope again, but some way down Butler lost his footing and slipped a considerable distance. He was not hurt, but the damage to his breeches was not slight, and when we gained our permanent camp where the horses were I had to patch them up to make him at all presentable.[15]

After returning to Mesopotamia the second time, they waited until Baker could ride into Christchurch and back again (the account does not say whether or not to fetch a new pair of breeches for Butler); then on January 31 they began a three-day journey (via the Clent Hills Station near Lake Heron) to the foot of the pass they had seen from the height above the Lawrence. It lay up Louper Stream (then unnamed), one of the uppermost tributaries of the Rakaia:

We pitched our camp and the next morning climbed to the top of the pass [this would make the actual date of the first crossing February 3, 1861] without any difficulty and went some distance down the other side till we were about twenty miles from the Coast, but found the whole valley so densely timbered that the chance of finding open country seemed hopeless. We therefore reluctantly retraced our steps to the top of the pass and began our descent, our only trouble being that a branch of the stream we were going down, which we had crossed earlier by jumping from rock to rock had so increased in volume from the melting snow that we had a thorough ducking on the return journey. However, as we regained our camp in a few hours, this mishap did not matter much. We had found 10,000 acres of inferior country up the Rakaia and later applied for this to the Land Board and secured it, but as it was never stocked the claim lapsed.[16]

After reaching the Clent Hills Station again, they separated, and the Erewhon journey had been completed. In the last year of Butler's life they met again in Rome, quite by accident. Meanwhile, Baker had gone on to numerous other exploits both in South and North Islands. He left New Zealand permanently in 1896 and died some thirty years later.

In actuality, thus, the Erewhon journey was made in two distinct starts from Mesopotamia, since the crossing above the Lawrence into the Rakaia Valley could not be made on horseback. The last two of the three separate rides and reconnoiterings afoot have been combined, with some editing, in *Erewhon.* From Mesopotamia, then, let us say, Higgs and Chowbok set out for the upper Rangitata even as Butler and John Holland Baker set out in January, 1861. They picked their way along the banks of the Rangitata, sometimes traveling more in the bed of the river itself than on what could be called its banks, crossed the Rangitata-Clyde, and proceeded on up the Lawrence. Leaving the headwaters of the Lawrence they crossed over to the headwaters of a much larger stream, the Rakaia, and from this point it would be easy enough to do precisely what is narrated in *Erewhon:* "We followed every stream but one, and always found it lead us to a glacier which was plainly impassable, at any rate without a larger party and ropes."[17] There are glaciers all about—Lyell, Ramsay, and others, feeding their icy and milky waters into the Rakaia. The one remaining stream is Louper Stream, which leads to Whitcombe Pass. Here we are thirty miles almost due north of Mesopotamia, but much farther, of course, by any ground route. Butler and Baker, looking for sheep country, discovered Whitcombe Pass but went down only a short distance on the other side: "too rough to go down without more help than we had." That a hope for gold, though a side issue, was always present Butler suggests in *The Fair Haven:*

The seeing of truth is as the finding of gold in far countries, where the shepherd has drunk of the stream and used it daily to cleanse the sweat of his brow, and recked little of the treasure which lay abundantly concealed therein, until one luckier than his fellows espies it, and the world comes flocking thither.[18]

As Pascoe says, "The vivid narrative in *Erewhon* is accurate." The route is shorn of side branches, such as the short penetration up the Clyde and the doubling back via Lake Heron, but even these are provided for in a general way. When the saddle and the statues are reached, reality gives way to fancy and Higgs finds what Butler and many other land-hungry squatters hoped to find but never did.

Erewhon Revisited affords, in abbreviated form, the same impressions. One of the more remarkable things about the long-delayed sequel is the proof it offers that Butler retained his New Zealand experiences in their pristine freshness. The journey to the pass drops naturally into the old images and idiom: the "D's" on his saddle, the billy for tea (the term is etymologized for the reader), the shepherd's talk of a "great fresh," the notation of tangled growth still unburnt— all this after nearly forty years of absence. New Zealand had sunk so profoundly into his memory (as any pioneering experience must) that it was easy enough for him to light his pipe—not on the shingle of the Rangitata but at 15 Clifford's Inn—and feel that

There was the clear starlit sky, the rushing river, and the stunted trees on the mountain-side; the woodhens cried, and the "more-pork" hooted out her two monotonous notes exactly as they had done years since; one moment, and time had so flown backwards that youth came bounding back to him with the return of his youth's surroundings.[19]

He is able to revive substantially the same natural intimacy that characterizes the early chapters of *Erewhon*. John Holland Baker tells us that

129

at the time of their reunion in 1902 Butler "had a wonderful memory, and mentioned many incidents and conversations I had forgotten years before."[20]

In another portion of *Erewhon Revisited,* the town of Fairmead suggests Ferrymead, though its population more closely approximates Lyttelton's. By the same token, Sunch'ston is Christchurch, and the temple might possibly have been suggested by Christchurch Cathedral, nearing completion in the late 1890's. How much Butler was aware of the history of the cathedral is conjectural, but there was more than enough about it in *The Press* during the 1860's, and it probably stuck in his mind enough to be recalled in subsequent conversations with visiting friends: Haast, the younger Reeves, and others. "The country between Sunch'ston and Fairmead," says *Erewhon Revisited,* was

. . . still mountainous, and being well wooded as well as well watered, abounded in views of singular beauty; but I have no time to dwell on the enthusiasm with which my father described them to me. The road took him at right angles to the main road down the valley from Sunch'ston to the capital, and this was one reason why he had chosen Fairmead rather than Clearwater, which was the next town lower down on the main road. He did not, indeed, anticipate that any one would want to find him, but whoever might so want would be more likely to go straight down the valley than to turn aside towards Fairmead.[21]

All this suggests a kind of blending of Ferrymead and Lyttelton, with "views of singular beauty" toward the sea, mountains, and plains.

Past the limits of immediate personal experience, the tone of both the Erewhon narratives undergoes a change. The plains of Erewhon have been said to be drawn from those of Lombardy, though the Canterbury Plains themselves (with which Butler in *A First Year* compares the plains of Lombardy) would serve equally well. With New Zealand scenery fundamentally in his mind, and with prime sheep country as the intended goal of both the real and the imaginary Erewhon journeys, it is rather natural to suppose that Butler (with a penchant for reversals) would transfer the Canterbury Plains to Westland

and allow himself to descend from the pass through territory he had seen many times and no doubt admired as sheep country, coming finally to Christchurch (Coldharbour—Sunchildston). But in any event, the description is quite perfunctory: we see "large pine forests," a "noble river," many "villages and hamlets." Higgs sinks upon the ground beneath nothing more specific than "a large tree," and the brief account of what the country looks like takes us no farther than the most banal variety of calendar lithograph. Butler is now much less interested in the country than in its people—who resemble in several interesting respects the better representatives of Chowbok's race, the Maoris.

EREWHON: ETHNOLOGY

*There are few Maoris here; they inhabit the north
island; and are only in small numbers, and degenerate in this, so may be passed over unnoticed. The
only effectual policy in dealing with them is to show
a bold front and, at the same time, do them a good
turn whenever you can be quite certain that your
kindness will not be misunderstood as a symptom
of fear.*

A FIRST YEAR IN CANTERBURY SETTLEMENT

The visitor to New Zealand is immediately impressed by the
amount of respect and prestige accorded the Maoris, who form
now only about 5 per cent of the total population. He learns, in time,
that some of this is ceremonial; that there is not invariably a perfect
accord between races, particularly when the Maoris are in the majority,
as they are in a few parts of North Island. But when all is said and
done, New Zealand's title to fame for her enlightened native policies
is well earned and secure.

The Maoris themselves, it must be remembered, had something to
do with creating and fostering this spirit of toleration. They were a
brave people, and uncommonly astute. They shared with Captains Tasman and Cook the distinction of discovery and exploration; they were
in New Zealand by choice and by virtue of superior seamanship. The

132

final impression they leave is profound: here was a Stone Age people possessing the arts of shipbuilding, navigation, fortification, agriculture, music, the dance, intricate carving and tattooing, storytelling. They could work a very hard green jade into ornaments and charms, and their bird snares and fishing arrangements were most ingenious. Along with all this went a fierceness that spent itself in raids, butcheries, and cannibal feasting upon the slain. They enslaved one another, and though until the *pakeha* came they had no alcohol, many of them were ugly enough when sober. Others were amazingly high-minded; there is plenty in local history, one soon discovers, to support both the noble-savage and the degraded-barbarian points of view.

The Maoris arrived in New Zealand from portions of Polynesia far north and east and hence much warmer. As a result, they preferred the comparatively "subtropical" portions of North Island. There were, however, a number of tribes that established themselves on South Island, which was the source of their much-prized greenstone, or jade. The way for white settlement on South Island had been partially prepared by the "Maori Napoleon," Te Rauparaha, whose raids decimated the Southern tribes earlier in the century just after muskets had reached Maori hands. Thus, though South Island was technically Maori domain the same as North Island, the presence of relatively few natives made the purchase and appropriation of land much easier for squatters. Furthermore, there was no possibility of a Maori resistance movement such as flared in the North during the 1860's. By Butler's time the Maoris both North and South had become "civilized" to the extent that they were no longer cannibals. Such statements as Henderson's, apropos of the possibility of Butler's being shipwrecked on North Island shortly after his departure in 1864—"The wind was so high that it broke the main yard clean in half, and had they been driven ashore they would in all probability have been killed and eaten, for the Maoris were still cannibals."[1]—would be hooted at in New Zealand by Maori and *pakeha* alike. South Island natives, as *Erewhon* quite correctly states, were "few in number" and "of an intelligent tractable disposition."

133

Butler says comparatively little about the Maoris, though he must have heard a good deal—from his friend Fitzgerald, for instance—and read about them in numerous places, including *The Press*. Edward Chudleigh's diary records the presence of a half-caste Maori at Butler's station, more than likely one of a mustering or shearing crew: with this man of "enormous strength" but "beautiful temper" the diarist had a "set to with the gloves for the edification of the station," with Butler no doubt among the edified. In *A First Year* Butler describes the South Island natives as "almost a thing of the past" and "degenerate—hardly worth notice."[2] The South Sea Islanders, on the other hand, he later links with the modern Italians and the ancient Greeks and Romans as "the most vigorous and amiable of known nations"— "nice people [who] have not as a general rule been purists."[3] From those who knew the Maoris somewhat better, he had the assurance that it would be safer to live among the heathen than among tribes so recently Christianized. In *Life and Habit* he remarks briefly upon the gradual extermination of the Indians in the United States, the aborigines in Australia, and the Maoris in New Zealand. The Alpine Italians' way of handling fire sets him to thinking about what he had known firsthand years previously.[4]

There is still in New Zealand an ambivalent attitude about the Maori that is evident in Butler. On the one hand, the Maori heritage is a source of pride with native and *pakeha* alike; but on the other hand, individual Maoris or even groups may occasionally be singled out as being degraded and as a degrading influence. There is still the question, too, of whether civilized life—urban life in particular—is really best for the Maori. However that may be, it is a matter of history that the Maori took to the imported tools and machinery very soon. Stone chisels for carving gave way to steel, though the carvings did not change appreciably. Other hand tools came into use, as well as European clothing (sometimes grotesquely worn, like the clothes of Professor Panky in *Erewhon Revisited*), and many Maoris became domestic servants or day-laborers. Augustus Earle's *Narrative* (1832) has left us an account of how the Maoris were attracted by new techniques.

Describing the landing at Te Horeke or "Deptford" on the Hokianga River, Earle says:

To me the most interesting circumstance was to notice the great delight of the natives, and the pleasure they seemed to take in observing the progress of the various works. All were officious to "lend a hand," and each seemed eager to be employed. This feeling corresponds with my idea of the best method of civilising a savage. Nothing can more completely show the importance of the useful arts than a dockyard. In it are practised nearly all the mechanical trades; and these present to the enquiring mind of a New Zealander a practical encyclopedia of knowledge. When he sees the combined exertions of the smith and carpenter create so huge a fabric as a ship, his mind is filled with wonder and delight; and when he witnesses the moulding of iron at the anvil, it excites his astonishment and emulation.[5]

One could hardly imagine the Maoris as a race that would become philosophically suspicious of machines. There was one machine, nevertheless, that by Butler's time had already proved their undoing: the musket. Not only were they on their way toward being exterminated by it—through their own intertribal wars, it should be added, not by the *pakeha* (not at first, that is)—but they were also subtly enslaved by it. Possession of muskets and powder, in self-defense, afforded a chance for survival; failure to secure them was tribal suicide, for none of the old weapons or tactics could stand before the terrible new guns. To secure firearms they must trade, and the traders drove bitter bargains: tons upon tons of tediously prepared flax for a few muskets, a small supply of powder. This was slavery to the machine in a very real sense, a kind of slavery the Maoris had never known. Earle notes the "dreadful effect" within the tribes, adding: "The whole soul of a New Zealander seems absorbed in the thoughts of war; every action of his life is influenced by it; and to possess weapons which give him such a decided superiority over those who have only their native implements of offence, he will sacrifice everything."[6] Whether Butler intended them or not, there are tragic undertones of the history of New Zealand in "The Book of the Machines."

The earliest accounts of dealings with the Maoris are somewhat Erewhonian in the same broad sense by which Butler seeks to give the impression of an untechnical people. For example, Polack's *New Zealand* relates—almost as an echo of *Gulliver's Travels*—an episode in which the Maoris are impressed by his watch. "This piece of mechanism," he says, "is called by the natives an Atua, or a divinity: few of my present audience had seen one, the ticking of which struck them with much surprise, which they evinced by repeated ejaculations."[7] And (as in the first visit to Erewhon) Polack's light complexion attracts attention.

Strangeness soon was accepted, however, and the Maoris found it to their advantage to be connected formally and regularly with a trader. This desire brought into existence a liaison class or caste which came to be known as the Pakeha Maori, a "Locksley Hall" figure who had literally acted upon his impulses:

> There the passions cramp'd no longer shall have
> scope and breathing space;
> I will take some savage woman, she shall rear
> my dusky race.

Before 1825, there were no more than a handful of Pakeha Maoris in all New Zealand, but by 1830 the number had increased to 50 and by 1835 to 100. At the peak—in 1840—there were 150, but by 1845 the number had dropped to 50 and by Butler's time there were few or none. Some did well for themselves; others simply "went bush" and disappeared from view. Dr. Arthur S. Thomson (source of the figures cited above) tells of finding traces of Pakeha Maoris here and there:

High up the Wanganui river a copy of Shakespeare, a classical dictionary, and a stone for grinding maize were shown to me by a chief, as the property of his former Pakeha Maori. On the banks of the Mokau river I stood upon the grave of one of these men, was shown a tattered English Prayer-book, the only property he left, and a half-caste girl gambolling in the river, the poor man's only child.[8]

136

Erewhon: *Ethnology*

What does *Erewhon* owe to the Maori and Maori tradition? First of all, some of its names. Conceivably, Butler's insistence that the name Erewhon itself be pronounced "as a word of three syllables, all short," is based on a recollection of Maori forms. Though no Maori word ends in a consonant, the *wh* spelling (the digraph is the only part of the word he did not reverse) is the representation of a bilabial *f*-type sound in Maori, and "Erewhone," with the addition of the final *e*, would make a euphonious pseudo-Maori word of the sort New Zealanders invent today ("Waikikamukau" with its bucolic implications is standard for American "Podunk"). The name "Arowhena" is closer still; there was a Maori settlement near the Waikato River (North Island) bearing the name spelled exactly as Butler has it. Johannes Andersen, an authority on Polynesian names, glosses "Arowhena" as one of the variant names of the highest mountain in Tahiti, and says—concerning a place name much nearer Butler's area and immediate experience— "It is not certain that the name *Arowhenua,* a Maori settlement with a considerable area of bush in the 'forties, but now a suburb of Temuka, South Canterbury, has anything to do with Arowhena."[9]

The name "Chowbok" (or "Kahabuka") appears to be pseudo-Maori, possibly not even pseudo. Though no *b* exists in standard Maori, there is evidence that the *p–b* variation (*tapu–tabu,* for instance) occurs in combinations. William Brown's *New Zealand and Its Aborigines* (1851) remarks on this, observing, "For instance, the native word for a vessel is *written* 'kai*p*uke,' but is very distinctly sounded kai*b*uke."[10] Brown thinks that the teaching of English would help improve the Maoris but asserts that the missionaries oppose it, saying that "the natives would only learn every species of vice through the medium of the English language."[11] If we were to follow Brown's phonology, we might come out with the interesting possibility of *kabupuka* > *kahabuka,* the first form meaning, among other things, "cabbagehead" (of the cabbage palm). One cannot insist on this rather fancy bit of etymologizing, which is probably too neat to be right, but it does seem evident that the name would have been appropriately

137

bestowed. A more reasonable conjecture, seeing that Chowbok becomes at the end of *Erewhon* "the Rev. William Habakkuk," is that *Kahabuka* is a Maorification of *Habakkuk;* but the name still awaits final elucidation. Aside from the foregoing, "Mahaina" seems to be the only other name to follow Maori or pseudo-Maori lines. "Chowbok" as a *pakeha* version of "Kahabuka," it should be added, offers one more example of the inveterate Anglo-Saxon indifference to the pronunciation of proper names which so cavalierly will convert a smooth murmur into a cough or a sneeze: thus Maori "Paraparaumu" has been reduced to "Pairpram," "Paekakariki" to "Pye-cock," and so forth. Periodically the New Zealand Broadcasting Service scolds the populace for living in phonetic sin.

The Erewhonian statues, readily recognizable as Polynesian, have been associated with the great stone figures of Easter Island with which they are congruent both in size and substance: "a circle of gigantic forms, many times higher than myself, upstanding grim and grey through the veil of cloud before me." Higgs later scales the size downward, but the statues remain quite large. In expression, however, they differ fundamentally, for the Easter Island figures are rather placid or stupid-looking, certainly not very sinister. The Erewhonian statues, on the other hand, bear a "super-humanly malevolent expression upon their faces," and, variously, are "raging furiously" or "lean and cadaverous with famine" or "cruel and idiotic, but with the silliest simper than can be conceived." Finally, "the mouths of all were more or less open."

Maori carving suits easily with most of these descriptions. It is never done in stone (except for greenstone *tikis,* on some of which an unsympathetic observer might readily detect a simper), but the well-carved meeting house is a riot of such grotesquerie as Butler describes. All, or virtually all, the figures are human but rendered in distortion; the mouths are all "more or less open" and the tongue protrudes; the arms, hands, and feet are variously contorted. Anyone encountering Maori carving for the first time imagines some of the sensations created

138

by Chowbok's trance, which is the counterpart of the trances of the Maori priest-artisan or *tohunga*:

In a moment his whole form was changed. His high shoulders dropped; he set his feet close together, heel to heel and toe to toe; he laid his arms and hands close alongside of his body, the palms following his thighs; he held his head high but quite straight, and his eyes stared right in front of him; but he frowned horribly, and assumed an expression of a face that was positively fiendish. At the best of times Chowbok was very ugly, but he now exceeded all conceivable limits of the hideous. His mouth extended almost from ear to ear, grinning horribly and showing all his teeth; his eyes glared, though they remained quite fixed, and his forehead was contracted with a most malevolent scowl.

I am afraid my description will have conveyed only the ridiculous side of his appearance; but the ridiculous and the sublime are near, and the grotesque fiendishness of Chowbok's face approached this last, if it did not reach it. I tried to be amused, but I felt a sort of creeping at the roots of my hair and over my whole body, as I looked and wondered what he could possibly be intending to signify. He continued thus for about a minute, sitting bolt upright, as stiff as a stone, and making this fearful face.[12]

Commenting on Maori carvings, George French Angas observed, in 1847,

The people of Easter Island—whose ancient inhabitants cut out of the soft volcanic rock huge statues, resembling the grotesque figures carved out of wood by the New Zealanders—more closely resemble the Maories than any other of the islanders of the Pacific: if we may credit the accounts given of them by former navigators.[13]

Though the Maoris did set up weird-looking carved posts around their *pas* (fortified villages) and occasionally produced oversized figures in wood, it is probably the most accurate to suppose that the Erewhonian statues are Maori in fierceness, Easter Island in bulk and in the fact that they are of stone. Neither, however, was designed to produce sound.

One further description (from Polack) of a Maori sepulchral post nearly thirty feet high may help round out the impression:

... the upper part [was] carved out into the resemblance of a man, with the ancient Egyptian sameness of expression standing on the head of a figure below with a grotesque face; the tongue, as is usual in the carvings of the native artists, was stretched as far as the material would allow the member to be extended; the eyes were formed of pieces of the pearl, paua, or mutton fish-shell, and were of sufficient dimensions to have supplied a host of figures; the knees were formed projecting outwards, and the feet were brought into one mass.[14]

Physically, then, it is not difficult to associate Polynesian fact with Butlerian fiction. Another aspect of the Maori background which had, indirectly, a good bit to do with *Erewhon* was the "lost tribes of Israel" theory with which Butler so gaily sports. This intrigued or amused him so much that he reverts to it in *Alps and Sanctuaries*; and in *The Way of All Flesh* he has Theobald and Christina bamboozled by impostors pretending to be Asiatic "actual living descendants of Jonadab, the son of Rechab." The lost-tribes theory is a common one, having been applied—on a not very scientific level—to all sorts of primitive races at the time of their discovery and early acquaintance. The idea that the Polynesians might be the lost tribes was broached as early as 1842 by the Right Rev. M. Russell, who in his *Polynesia: or, an Historical Account of the Principal Islands in the South Sea, including New Zealand* devoted his final chapter to exploring resemblances between the Polynesians and the Israelites, Greeks, and Romans. He finds clues in human sacrifice, infanticide, and self-laceration in mourning, and, warming to his subject, declares:

It requires no ingenuity to discover in the religious usages of the Polynesians such a resemblance to those of the other Asiatic nations as to afford the greatest possibility that they were sprung from the same source. In the practices every where prevailing, we perceive traces of that original faith which, though given to man by a divine agency, has perpetuated itself through a channel so corrupted as to have lost the sublime import and the purer ceremonies by means of which it first addressed itself to the acceptation of the descendants of Noah.[15]

But the position of the Right Rev. Mr. Russell is pallid by comparison with that of another clergyman, the Rev. Richard Taylor, M.A., F.G.S., who in 1855 produced a book called *Te Ika a Maui* [Maui's Fish]; *or New Zealand and Its Inhabitants.*

There is a South Island legend of a lost tribe of Maoris themselves—the Ngatimamoe, who after being all but exterminated by the Kaitahu, disappeared into the mountains and were seen no more. Until comparatively recent times, the belief has existed that the Ngatimamoe might some day be found; such a legend in itself lent a certain mystery to the portion of New Zealand in which *Erewhon* is laid. However, it remained for the Rev. Mr. Taylor to embrace the whole Maori population with the theory that they were the Ten Lost Tribes. His book, a voluminous effort, is generally sympathetic with the Maoris; it praises them for "good feeling and kindliness one towards another," for "careful avoiding [of] all sorts of quarrels," and "powerful emotions of joy, on meeting with absent friends." Taylor interprets such native institutions as the *tapu* as being suited to primitive circumstances, and of the race in general he remarks:

Naturally a noble race, bodily and mentally superior to most of the Polynesians, their fine intelligent countenances present the exterior of a fair-built house, which only requires to be suitably furnished, and we may hope that they have already passed through the worst part of that transition state which, under less favourable circumstances, it took centuries to bring our own country through, to attain its present highly advanced position in the scale of nations.[16]

He shows, however, that he devotedly believes this race to be the lost tribes—perhaps because they *are* "naturally a noble race." The Introduction speaks of the inhabitants of the Chatham Islands (the Morioris, driven out of New Zealand by the Maoris) as "an instance to what sad state man may fall"—a reminder of the depravity of the prodigal son:

141

May not this beautiful parable have its literal fulfilment in the history of the New Zealand race; in it may we not behold one of the long lost tribes of Israel, which, with its fellows, having abandoned the service of the true God, and cast aside his Word, fell step by step in the scale of civilization; deprived of a fixed home, became nomad wanderers over the steppes of Asia, a bye-word and a reproach among the nations, and gradually retreated until in the lapse of ages they reached the sea, and thence, still preserving their wandering character, from island to island driven by winds and currents, and various causes, they finally reached New Zealand, and there fallen to their lowest state of degradation, given up to the fiercest passions, consumed, and being consumed, they are enabled to reflect, repent, and amend, and resolve to arise and go to their Father.[17]

In his chapter on language, Taylor notes similarities of Maori to Coptic, Egyptian, East Indian, and other languages. Easter Island, with its statues, is suggested as "the abode of the progenitors of the Polynesian race before it had lost some of its original knowledge of the arts":

The large stone monuments still existing there, speak of a bygone skill, and, perhaps, of acquaintance with the use of iron. The form, too, of the covering of the heads of those figures bears a remarkable resemblance to those seen in Egyptian hieroglyphics, especially of that supposed to refer to Shishak's victory over Rehoboam.[18]

Taylor leaves fine points in language to the specialists but still "ventures to hint" that

. . . the many points of resemblance in feature, general customs, and manners, may enable us to discover in the widely spread Polynesian race, a remnant of the long-lost tribes of Israel, and when the time arrives for their restoration from all countries in which they have been dispersed, from "Hamath and the Isles of the Sea" that, in that day it will be found, even to these ends of the world, the fearful denunciation of Divine wrath has driven his apostate people, who, forsaking the true light given them, and preferring heathen darkness, until they had fulfilled their appointed times.[19]

The ten tribes, he thinks, may have dispersed over Asia and at length arrived in Polynesia: "There is no saying where they may not have gone." Appendix A to his book contains "A list of New Zealand customs resembling those alluded to in Scripture as being common in Israel, or to the heathen around them, for conformity to many of which they were driven from their inheritance." There is a total of thirty-six, including the cutting of flesh for grief, tattooing, hair used in sacrifice, touching of food, and bulrush vessels.

It appears quite likely that the Reverend Russells and Taylors (of whom there may have been several more) supplied Butler's motivation for the pious concern Higgs exhibits over the Erewhonians as the lost tribes. This would tend also to identify the Erewhonians more closely with the higher-type Maoris, so much admired by Taylor and numerous other observers. The lost-tribes motif adds just the right touch of officious absurdity to the character of Higgs besides helping, unconsciously but quite materially, to set the stage for *Erewhon Revisited*. Further, it offers a satiric counterweight to the crass proposal of Christian slavery for Polynesians, advanced at the end of the book.

Butler's ridicule of clerical associations with the Maoris extended past such speculations; on the whole he seems to have understood pretty well, as a professionally trained clergyman himself, the tenuous character of Maori Christianity. He uses Chowbok to illustrate the folly of assuming too fast an assimilation to European religion. Writing in *The Reasoner* soon after his return to England, he said:

Sydney Smith said well, that when a missionary wrote home from India of his having made so many converts to Christianity, the chances were he had only spoiled that number of Hindoos, and I have heard it stated by those who have lived long among the New Zealand Maoris that they would rather trust their life and honour with the only remaining heathen tribe than with those who had been made Christian.[20]

Chowbok is quite plainly a "spoiled Maori": he is not to be trusted, and yet at the end of *Erewhon* we find him doing very nicely as "the Rev. William Habakkuk" and at the end of *Erewhon Revisited*, no less a personage than a bishop! The Otago Museum at Dunedin owns

143

an oil painting entitled "The New Zealand Chiefs in Wesley's House," done by James Smetham in 1863. One of the figures could easily have been "the Rev. William Habakkuk."*

Chowbok's being "a great liar" seems not to invalidate other estimates of native character. W. Tyrone Power, for example, points out that though Maoris are generally trustworthy and honest, they have flexible ideas of the truth:

It is a pity they do not extend the same condemnation [of thievery] to lying, which is an almost universal failing, and is considered no disgrace whatever. They have not even the Spartan virtue of being ashamed when found out, and cannot comprehend the advantage of repressing the vagaries of a romantic imagination. The consequence is, that the natives are generally distrustful and incredulous; and "toe" and "teto," lie and liar, are the words most frequently used in their conversation, and which they apply to one another and to white men of all ranks without the least hesitation or compunction, and are greatly surprised at the indignation evidenced by the latter at such an accusation.[21]

On the other hand, for Chowbok to accompany Higgs accorded with best practice in the earliest days of back-country exploration. Maoris were frequently consulted about local geography; and when Harper and Locke made the first crossing to the West Coast in 1857 they did so only with the help of a Maori guide, Ihaia Tainui. They found some gold on this first trip, but the main gold-fever in Canterbury did not come until 1864/65. Active prospecting, however, had already begun, in 1860, at the time Butler was exploring.

Chowbok and Higgs, far up in the mountains by their campfire, are recalled by a passage in *Alps and Sanctuaries*:

The New Zealand Maoris say the white man is a fool: "He makes a large fire, and then has to sit away from it; the Maori makes a small fire, and sits over it." The scheme of an Italian kitchen-fire is that there shall be one

---

* That Chowbok was even a Maori has not always been accepted; one writer, for instance, in the *Papers of The Bibliographical Society of America,* refers to him as an "untrust-worthy Indian" and the "Indian guide."

144

stout log smouldering on the hearth, from which a few live coals may be chipped off if wanted, and put into the small square gratings which are used for stewing or roasting. Any warming up, or shorter boiling, is done on the Maori principle of making a small fire of light dry wood, and feeding it frequently.[22]

The portrait of Chowbok exhausts Butler's attention to the Maori recognizable either as individual or type, but *Erewhon* contains considerably more that is referable to Maori culture. Most of the early accounts available to Butler include descriptions of the *tapu* (taboo), a system of prohibitions which was by no means peculiar to the Maoris but was rigidly enforced among them. Several observers assert that the *tapu* in operation is much less capricious and tyrannical than it seems in the abstract; that as a social system it does work to preserve stability. Taylor called it "a remarkable institution" which under prevailing circumstances was "politic and wise."[23] The *pakeha* knew, and for the most part respected, the most important *tapu*'s: certain portions of ground remained undeveloped, certain mountains remained for a time unclimbed, by virtue of their being *tapu*. There are remnants of the system still to be encountered in New Zealand.

All Erewhon was *tapu* country so far as Chowbok was concerned; and the Erewhonians had, in effect, placed a *tapu* on machinery. Butler describes it as a less mystical procedure, but the result is stated in much the same terms as the operation of the *tapu*: a violation is met with expressions of horror and hostility of the kind that a primitive tribe might show:

. . . the Erewhonians are a meek and long-suffering people, easily led by the nose, and quick to offer up common sense at the shrine of logic, when a philosopher arises among them, who carries them away through his reputation for especial learning, or by convincing them that their existing institutions are not based on the strictest principles of morality.[24]

This characterization of the Erewhonians (added late, in the 1901 edition) does not fit the Maoris altogether on the score either of meekness or of susceptibility to philosophical argument, but the *tapu* was certainly conceived of as conforming with the "strictest principles of morality." Dr. Thomson even suggested a parallel with England:

The New Zealand system of Tapu will bear comparison with the laws flourishing in England not a thousand years ago. Does there not exist occasionally in the present day a belief in the divine right of kings and of certain priests? Several laws enforced by the New Zealand tapu are in accordance with the seventh commandment. Tapuing seeds and fields are types of the English laws for protecting out-door property; women tapued to men is matrimony; tapuing sick persons is analogous to the quarantine orders against lepers, the plague and the yellow fever. Every tapu relating to the dead is a law against sacrilege, and tapuing rivers and lands to annoy enemies finds a parallel in the modern system of blockade.[25]

An earlier writer, Augustus Earle, offers a parallel to the Erewhonian consumptive: after describing the effects of tuberculosis on the Maoris, Earle says: "They never attempt any means of curing or alleviating the pains caused by this cruel complaint; and all those under its influence are tabooed."[26]

The whole Maori medical practice, or rather absence of practice, fits the Erewhonian pattern. Disease remained untreated because it was regarded as a visitation of the gods—a form of moral sanction to be associated logically with the *tapu*. Edward Shortland (an M.A. from Cambridge and Extra-Licentiate of the Royal College of Surgeons) gave this explanation in 1851:

The spirits of his departed ancestors, jealous of the infringement of their "ritenga" or rites, will commission some spirit of their kin to enter into his body, and feed on some vital part. The visible signs of this hidden and mysterious process they believe to be the various forms of disease. The mildest forms of disease are hence supposed to be caused by the spirits of those who knew the sufferer while on earth, and are therefore imagined to be more merciful, and more reluctant to injure an old friend and relation: the worst forms are supposed to be caused by the spirit of a dead infant, who, having never contracted any affection for those on earth, tears and feeds on the vitals of his nearest kin without compunction.[27]

Not to multiply Erewhonian parallels unduly, it might be remarked in passing that this plaguing of mortals by dead infants bears a more than casual resemblance to "The World of the Unborn."

Butler did well to keep his Erewhonians on a simple level, and his acquaintance with Maori custom appears to have been just sufficient to let him view it in terms of satiric possibilities. If we did not see the Erewhonians as semisavages, intellectually speaking, we would lose some of the satiric force, for *Erewhon* suggests to us that we too are Erewhonians in some of our ways.

Even more striking than the Erewhonian prohibitions, however, are the punishments and the social deviations punished. Here we come upon another Polynesian parallel which for Butler's purpose is more useful than the *tapu*. This is *muru*—the ceremonial plundering of the unfortunate. The early accounts of the Maoris speak very frequently of *muru* as well as *tapu*, the two often being taken together as cardinal features of a bizarre social system. The most relevant account of many that might be cited comes from a book entitled *Old New Zealand*, by "A Pakeha Maori" (F. E. Maning, who lived among the Maoris for years). This book, fully deserving a high reputation among Antipodean readers of the present day (it should be more widely known outside New Zealand and Australia than it is), came to the attention of *The Press* in March of 1863, the year of its first publication. It is quite unlikely that Butler would have overlooked an extensive review appearing in the *Press* on March 28, 30, and 31, especially since his own letters on Darwinism were appearing concurrently: the review falls midway in the series. *Old New Zealand* was later advertised as being on sale in the *Press* office.

That Butler may have been indebted to Judge Maning (the Pakeha Maori became a lawyer and jurist of some fame after his return to civilization) was suggested some twenty-odd years ago (March 17, 1934) by "A. B.," writing in the *Press* itself on "Erewhonian Ideas."[28] "Can it have been [asks A. B.] the custom of *muru* which first set Butler thinking on these lines?" The reasoning continues:

Trails into Erewhon

The beginnings of "Erewhon" date from 1863, the year in which Maning's "Old New Zealand" first appeared. The chapters which concern us, however, do not seem to have been written before 1870. Maning's book does not fail to bring out what Butler would call the "nice" side of the Maori people, though it does not conceal their savagery; and its excellence was such as must make an impression on Butler, as it does on its readers to-day.*

The *Press* review of 1863 devotes slightly more than a column to re-printing Maning's account of *muru* and *tapu*, explaining *muru* as a "regular legalized and established custom of plundering as penalty for offences, which in a way resemble[s] our law by which a man is obliged to pay 'damages.' " The examples are briskly presented:

The offences for which people were plundered were sometimes of a nature which, to a *mere* pakeha, would seem curious. A man's child fell in the fire, and was almost burnt to death. The father was immediately plundered to an extent that almost left him without the means of subsistence: fishing nets, canoes, pigs, provisions, all went. His canoe upset, and he and all his family narrowly escaped drowning—some were, perhaps, drowned. He was immediately robbed, and well pummelled with a club into the bargain, if he was not good at the science of self-defence—the club part of the ceremony being always fairly administered one against one, and after fair warning given to defend himself. He might be clearing some land for potatoes, burning off the fern, and the fire spreads farther than he intended, and gets into a *wahi tapu,* or burial ground. No matter whether any one has been buried in it or not for the last hundred years, he is tremendously robbed; and I can really imagine a case in which a man for scratching his own head might be legally robbed.[29]

The explanation goes on to say that *muru* is never questioned or resisted; in fact it "would have been felt as a slight, and even an insult,

---

* The same article points out a similarity between "The Book of the Machines" and Disraeli's *Coningsby* (Bk. IV, ii), in which Coningsby, visiting Manchester, contemplates the machines there and argues that they breathe, have voices, reproduce, and are generally enough like human beings (or superior to them) to "fill the mind with curious and even awful speculation."

not to be robbed," and to resist *"would have debarred the contemptible individual from the privilege of robbing his neighbours . . ."* *

Here we have an ethnological basis for the absurdities of Erewhon; Mr. Nosnibor, for the "misfortune" of having embezzled money in a "severe fit of immorality" is put on bread and water and flogged once a week by the straightener, just as the Maori father whose child fell in the fire was plundered. In the 1901 edition of *Erewhon*, Butler both expanded his explanation and indicated his familiarity with *muru*:

> The strange part of the story, however, is that though they ascribe moral defects to the effect of misfortune either in character or surroundings, they will not listen to the plea of misfortune in cases that in England meet with sympathy and commiseration only. Ill luck of any kind, or even ill treatment at the hands of others, is considered an offence against society, inasmuch as it makes people uncomfortable to hear of it. Loss of fortune, therefore, or loss of some dear friend on whom another was much dependent, is punished hardly less severely than physical delinquency.
>
> Foreign, indeed, as such ideas are to our own, traces of somewhat similar opinions can be found even in nineteenth-century England. . . . Among foreign nations Erewhonian opinions may be still more clearly noted. The Mahommedans, for example, to this day, send their female prisoners to hospitals, and the New Zealand Maories visit any misfortune with forcible entry into the house of the offender, and the breaking up and burning of all his goods. The Italians, again, use the same word for "disgrace" and "misfortune."[30]

On the more strictly *pakeha* side of things, it might have seemed also that being fined for scab in sheep was one form of *muru*; certainly the fact of scab itself was a misfortune of the first order. A man's flock might be virtually wiped out by scab, which explains the necessity of fines running at times into hundreds of pounds. A fine of £200, for instance, was levied against Shepherd's Bush, a station down the north bank of the Rangitata from Mesopotamia, in 1862; and at Whiterock,

---

* Italics are Maning's.

in another portion of the province, there were fines of £1,000 and £1,500 in the sixties.[31]

But to return to Maning, there is special interest in a suggestion of his that would apply Maori custom to English law:

> The above slight sketch of the penal law of New Zealand I present and dedicate to the Law Lords of England, as it might, perhaps, afford some hints for a reform in our own. The only remark I shall have to add is, that if a man killed another, "malice prepense aforethought," the act, in nineteen cases out of twenty, would be either a meritorious one, or of no consequence whatever; in either of which cases the penal code had, of course, nothing to do in the matter. If, however, a man killed another by accident, in the majority of cases the consequences would be most serious; and not only the involuntary homicide, but every one connected with him would be plundered of everything they possessed worth taking. This however, to an English lawyer, may require some explanation. . . .[32]

This is all but a command invitation for someone to start writing *Erewhon.* And in *Old New Zealand* there is abundance of satire and dry humor of the kind that Butler relished. If he needed a hint toward the invertedness of Erewhon, Maning was ready with it and in part (more than likely) showed him the way to use it; his is the tone it needed. Maning's exuberance is like Mark Twain's, but his eye for incongruities and ironies is like Butler's. Broome may have given Butler "the final shove into *Erewhon,*" but Maning helped lead him to the brink just as surely as Chowbok took him up to the saddle.

Thus far, we have been obliged to see the more curious and—to the European eye—more fantastic side of Maori life. It is what interested Butler most as a satirist and what enters most largely into *Erewhon.* It is already apparent, though, that he admired the Maoris in some respects, and we shall see that the last few pages of *Erewhon* are an indictment of colonial native policy. South Island could no doubt take a comparatively dispassionate view of the war that began in North Island in 1860 and was still raging when Butler left for England. Having few natives to deal with and enjoying much less complicated access to native (or lately native) lands, South Islanders could easily come to feel that the war was morally wrong, as indeed historians more than once have said it was. *The Press* inveighed editorially against it on numerous occasions, and was quick to respond to the heroism of the Maoris at Maungatautari—New Zealand's Thermopylae or Alamo. Its editorial of April 16, 1864, sums up the case with eloquence befitting the subject:

AKE! AKE! AKE!

"For Ever—For ever—For ever." Three hundred men lay within the rude defence round which some fifteen hundred British troops were posted. Artillery was playing on the palisades, and a flying sap had been run up to the foot of the field work. Without food or water they waited the final assault, when the messengers of peace made them the last offer—their lives and good treatment if they would but surrender to a fate which was inevitable. No human situation can be conceived more desperate or more hopeless—their lands gone, their race melting away like snow before the sun, and now their own time come at last; with enemies surrounding them on all sides, and nothing but certain death staring them in the face, this is the last answer which they give to a proposal of peace and surrender, "Friends,—this is the reply of the Maori: We will go on fighting for ever! for ever! for ever!" We make bold to say that in whatever tongue the colonisation of the New Zealand Islands by the Anglo-Saxons be written, this reply, of the last of the Waikatos will be told for a memorial of them; and men will ask in after times, was it good to destroy a race who could so defend their native land? There certainly does seem to be a sort of curse upon our army in this unhappy conflict. Why is it, that we who boast of possessing the chivalry of the civilised world,—we with our guns and mortars, our rifles and bayonets, our ships of war, and gunboats, and steamers, above all, our boundless commissariat,—why is it that we have now for these four years fought these naked, half-armed tribes, living on bruised corn, putrid sharks, and potatoes, with their old fowling-pieces and their threadbare blankets, and that, not in mountain fastnesses and trackless forests, but in the open country, where our horse-artillery can travel, and by the side of rivers which our steamers can traverse, and yet

151

can hardly win an advantage, except by large superiority of force? Why is it, that, as at Maungatautari, it takes us fifteen hundred men to beat three hundred Natives? and that even then we suffer a loss of nearly seventy men killed and wounded,—nearly one fourth of the whole force of the enemy? Why is it, that where one hundred British soldiers go out to attack the enemy, as at Taranaki, they are broken, shot down, dispersed, and driven in utter rout from the field by two or three hundred naked savages? We are not accustomed to read of these things in the history of English warfare. We venture to say that in all the annals of our race no similar passage can be found so little honorable to the British arms as that of the War in New Zealand. There seems some strange kind of paralysis on all our attempts. We are making efforts and incurring an expenditure sufficient to conquer powerful and civilised communities. With a less force nation after nation in the Indian Peninsula has bowed before us, and poured the treasured wealth of centuries into the lap of the conquerors. We can fight Russians one to twenty on the heights of Inkerman, or Sepoys one to a hundred on the plains of India, but here we meet the Native New Zealander, and go out against him as if he were a jungle tiger with armed hosts, and even then, witness by our loss, the difficulty of the conquest. We ask, why is it that so strange a blight has come over our arms? We know not. But this we know—there will be men in after times whose pens will narrate the causes and outcomings of this contest, and who will seek, in the objects of the war, the key to its disasters. They will say it was not a war for safety or for law, or for truth or liberty, but it was a war dictated by avarice and prosecuted for spoliation. It was a war to remove a neighbour's land mark—to destroy a race that we might dwell in their tents. No doubt these critics of the past will be wrong. They must be so; for is not the whole voice of the age against them? An enlightened, christian, money-making people, we are quite satisfied with the morality of our own conduct; but still the events of the war remain unexplained. Still it will remain to be solved why more money, time, and life, should have been sacrificed in this war against a feeble foe, for a smaller result than in any war in which England has ever yet engaged. For our own parts, we have long ceased to speculate on the causes of these things; we wait and wonder. But if there be any thing in the whole miserable story to excite the admiration of a generous mind, it is the sad spectacle of those grim and tawny figures, gaunt with the watching and weariness, the wounds and nakedness of a long campaign in the bush, staring over their ragged palisades on the hosts of the conquerors from whom escape was impossible, and wailing out their last chant of death and defiance—ake, ake, ake—for ever! for ever! for ever![33]

Some of this indignation must have passed over to Butler, as easily it might, for when in the conclusion to *Erewhon* he comes to contemplate the colonial attitude toward natives, nothing short of Swiftian irony will serve him. In "Modest Proposal" fashion he hatches a scheme whereby he will "guarantee that I will convert the Erewhonians not only into good Christians but into a source of considerable profit to the shareholders." To add weight, he quotes from the London *Times* an account of Polynesian serfs in Queensland—Australia being then as now less qualmish than New Zealand in its exploitation of native labor. Coolly he points out that a gunboat could round up and subdue cargoes of slaves (though he is careful not to use the word "slave") : "the supply of Erewhonians would be unlimited, and they could be packed closely and fed at a very reasonable cost."[34]

The reference to the gunboat suggests still another link with the Maori wars: the river up which it is to be sent "descends from the Snowy Mountains, and passes through Erewhon, [and] is known to be navigable for several hundred miles from its mouth"—a proper stream for gunboat traffic. This comes very close to describing not a South Island river but the Waikato River of North Island, which (as the *Press* editorial points out) British gunboats actually did ascend to assist the troops against the Maoris. The unarmed Erewhonians, ignorant of gunpowder, would hardly parallel the Maori rebels of the 1860's; but the natives were at a murderous disadvantage in equipment. Sentiment being what it was in Christchurch, it seems likely enough that Higgs's scheme for the evangelization of Erewhon by what *The Press* sarcastically designated "an enlightened, christian, money-making people" is a satiric afterthought directed at colonial policy in New Zealand and Australia alike.

The proposition goes on to argue that religious instruction to the captives would compensate everyone all round: the Erewhonians would be Christianized and their masters' consciences set at ease:

> This must be insisted upon, both in order to put a stop to any uneasy feeling which might show itself either in Queensland or in the mother country as to the means whereby the Erewhonians had been obtained, and also because it would give our shareholders the comfort of reflecting that they were saving souls and filling their own pockets at one and the same moment.[35]

And now that Higgs has convinced himself that the company is not only feasible but practically a moral duty, he is ready to soft-pedal the idea of the lost tribes:

> The first step would be to draw up a prospectus. In this I would advise that no mention should be made of the fact that the Erewhonians are the lost tribes. The discovery is one of absorbing interest to myself, but it is of a sentimental rather than commercial value, and business is business.[36]

Here again is the voice of anti-imperialism sounded earlier in the *Press*. England might grind the Maoris into surrender at last, but not without a lasting moral defeat. So might imperialism continue to ride high throughout the whole of New Zealand and Australia: its career could be followed in the columns of the *Times*. What could result other than progressive entanglement in a morally indefensible position? It might take the chickens a long time to come home to roost, but come they would—and did.

For *Erewhon* the native background proved enriching: it lent re-mote-sounding names, a grotesque art, a possibility of being piously regarded as the lost tribes of Israel, one full-length character in Chowbok, and a topsy-turvy code of morals. When an erstwhile squatter neighbor gave him the final shove, Butler was better prepared to land than he may have realized.

THE PROGENY OF *EREWHON*

*You will not forget the pretty roundness of my liter-
ary career!* α Erewhon, ω Erewhon Revisited.

—LETTER TO MR. AND MRS. FULLER MAITLAND,
MAY 14, 1902

A Wellington newspaper of the 1850's, describing one of Canterbury's delegates to the House of Representatives (Mr. John
Hall) noted the gentleman's curious habit of constantly rising on tip-
toe when speaking. The paper then

. . . went on to say that he [the writer] had noticed the same peculiarity in
other Canterbury members, and hazarded the conjecture that it arose through
the flatness of the Canterbury Plains, and the consequent necessity of a
strained attitude when looking for sheep among the tussocks![1]

While it would not quite do to assume that Butler developed either his
"strained attitude" or his tenacity in pursuing an idea through his role
as shepherd, it is nevertheless true that pioneering did give him a perception of hard fact and the resolution to deal with it. He succeeded
in New Zealand because of the close attention to detail which became
the hallmark of his life: the keeping of double-entry accounts, the
regularity of study at the British Museum, the punctilio of outward
deportment. It was his meticulous attention to the minutiae of theory

155

and text that trapped him, in fact, into his controversy with Darwin; for prone to imagine others as meticulous as himself, he erroneously concluded that what actually was careless or indifferent was deliberate and unscrupulous. Such respect for truth and lucidity, in nature, he had learned in an exacting school: those frontiersmen who survive are more often realists than not. Unquestionably, Butler matured and seasoned himself at Mesopotamia.

His formula for success had involved three distinct stages: first, finding the right location and securing it against encroachment; next, building up a homestead, stocking the run, and operating long enough to give the establishment solidness and continuity; and finally, choosing the time to sell at a good profit. At any one of these stages he could easily have met disaster; many men did.

The questing phase was easily the most entertaining and romantic. Undoubtedly Butler relished exploring, or he would hardly have undertaken more than the barest minimum necessary to his purposes. New Zealand offered him abundant opportunity. In the consummate descriptive prelude to *Erewhon* he distilled his mountaineering experiences into a narrative of progressive suspense and extraordinary conviction, helping immeasurably to conduct the reader into the satiric core of the book. In this kind of skill Butler resembles Swift not a little: the headstrong young explorer, Higgs, is fit companion for Lemuel Gulliver. Intellectually limited and somewhat naïve as both are made out to be, both at the same time are allowed to retain their fundamentally sensible humanity amidst a constellation of marvels. Both take things in stride and render their ingenuous reports from a viewpoint not much off center. Swift's imagination, coupled with his reading, created the plausible circumstances of Gulliver's several voyages—one of which, curiously enough, bordered geographically as well as mentally upon the region of Erewhon, for it took Gulliver to a latitude and longitude that would place him somewhere near the then-still-unknown center of Australia. Butler, fortuitously, required neither a background of reading nor a flight of fancy to get himself to the frontiers of Erewhon, but it is no small merit that he was able to seize upon the imaginative potential of what to most New Zealanders was everyday experience. Without the solid conviction carried through the early chapters, the book would have been immeasurably weaker. This shoring-up was the contribution of Mesopotamia.

But Canterbury, as we have seen, was not all one vast sheeppen for man and beast alike, without opportunity for diversion, and Butler made the most of Christchurch. We would like to know more than we do about his movements there, and especially more about his contributions to *The Press,* but the available evidence is enough to demonstrate that he made his mark in both town and country among men who were characteristically his peers and sometimes his superiors. "If," says Massingham, "it is a giant, objective paradox of Butler's life, detached from the conscious ironies of his mind, to find a man of such masterly intellectual power and intellectual preoccupations living rougher than the roughest not only as a colonist but in the pioneer days of colonial enterprise, it is certain that he could not have lived among these virgin ranges, just as a sheep-farmer and nothing more."[2] He was no Gulliver in Lilliput. The society of Canterbury offered a stimulus he could never have received, say, as a tutor at Cambridge—a stimulus he was to forfeit, moreover, by his return. Perhaps the duality is best described by the observation in his *Note-Books* that "common sense is the unalterable canto fermo and philosophy is the variable counterpoint." He had found room for both.

In both a historical and a contemporary sense, New Zealand represents a rather dramatic struggle for cultural survival, a grim resolution not to be overwhelmed by "the bush" on the one hand or pastoral ease on the other. Any frontier is a meeting place of extremes, productive of the material for literature, perhaps, but not of the best conditions for bringing it into being. That takes an act of will, and it is also will that over the years in New Zealand has placed a museum and gallery in each of the four principal cities and various cultural centers in smaller places; that has provided a broadcasting service which recognizes and rejoices in the existence of adult intelligence; that has saved generous reserves of its native flora for posterity; that has developed a sane and

157

equitable economy which puts reason and public interest above greed and exploitation. All the way along, New Zealand has been more empirical than theoretical, but empirical with a set of values always clearly in view.

After accumulating a modest but presumably competent fortune, Butler left New Zealand for England: for what? To mew himself up in Clifford's Inn and walk a sheep trail back and forth to the British Museum; to write one book that England would consent to read and to spend the rest of his days, and substantial sums of his capital, on others that it would largely ignore; to lose in speculations the "birthright" fortune he had won; to find stimulating friendship with one woman and to know few other individuals above mediocrity; to trap himself into scientific polemics that embittered and withered him; to anticipate the Handel revival, composing oratorios that were never heard. How could New Zealand, short of drowning him in the Rangitata, have served him worse? The colony held a wide circle of better friends than he ever came to know in England (other than Shaw) and —conceivably—better things for him to do. When he turned his back on New Zealand he cut himself off from the deepest creative urges he had known. Even for *Erewhon,* the needful encouragement was to come not from any London-bred literary acquaintance (though Miss Savage was soon to appear) but from one of his erstwhile squatter neighbors. Broome, it turned out, was a better judge of satiric literature than George Meredith, who recommended to Chapman & Hall that the manuscript be rejected. On the basis of the connection Butler was so fond of making between money and personality, it might be suggested that both he and his money fared worse upon removal than if they had remained.

It may be that Butler wondered, at times, whether he had gained or lost by coming "Home." At least he had cause enough to wonder. In his last years his thoughts reverted longingly toward New Zealand: he recalled his early friends there, several of whom he had met again in England or on the Continent, wrote letters, and sent copies of his books (including a set for the public library in Christchurch) to various New Zealanders. After his death the manuscript of *The Fair Haven* was dispatched to the same library, and a self-portrait delivered to Mr. O. T. J. Alpers with the request that it be placed in some institution where it would be seen. This, it appears, created something of a problem. According to *The Press* (April 11, 1936) the portrait reposed uneasily for a time with the Society of Arts; then

The officials discovered, somewhat belatedly, and with regret, that they were unable to accept the gift. A few tongues were raised in protest, but the Phillistines [*sic*] prevailed, and the picture of the man who wrote for posterity was hurried off to hang, in decent obscurity among the stuffed elephants and the grizzly bears, in the Canterbury museum.

Even in this retreat, however, there was no rest for the unorthodox. Where next to send him? Someone thought of the library, and the unwanted gift was offered, with open-hearted generosity, to the public library. Somewhat reluctantly, the library rose to the occasion. Face downward, in disgrace, the picture travelled along Rolleston avenue, down Hereford street, and in at the library doors. Thereafter, it lay hidden for some years till it was found, dusty and forgotten, in a cupboard, and elevated to a position on the walls of the reading room in the circulating department. Here, for some years, Samuel Butler mounted guard, regarding with his saturnine smile the readers of the current literature of the day.

Later still, the present chief librarian, Mr. E. J. Bell, rescued the portrait, and placed it in a position of honour in the reference library. For some time it hung between the pictures of two Canterbury philanthropists. Three years ago it was taken down, renovated, and hung in the new Robert McDougall Art Gallery.

The "saturnine" face must have regarded also the Ydgrunites of Christchurch: "Conformity," says *Erewhon*, "until absolutely intolerable is a law of Ydgrun."

"Butler's mind was so acute and powerful, so vivid and subtle," says Mrs. Stillman, one of his most discerning critics, "that whatever his life, he would probably have used it in some creative way, but the fact remains that his peculiar misfortunes were the very things that sharpened and stimulated his natural faculties and determined the material they should work on."³ This is a truth we sense vividly throughout Butler's New Zealand experience; his contemporaries in the colony could sense it in him too, except that they did not relate it to his misfortunes for the reason that these seemed at the time to lie behind him. He was in the ascendancy there, and we may imagine that he might easily have continued so. Was it a career in art that he most wanted? A painter with only a modest degree of originality and a high degree of resolution, working persistently in South Island during the latter nineteenth century, could have created or helped create for the region an artistic tradition many decades before any such tradition finally began to appear. Or had he been born, rather, to become a writer? This also he might have managed, unless we are to assume that colonial life was such as to throttle any genius, however well equipped and however much at leisure to pursue his aims. Such an assumption is not necessarily valid. It is idle enough, perhaps, and too easy, to speculate very extensively on "what might have been" for Butler as one person, but it is not idle to try to judge whether man and moment could have continued sufficient to each other in a situation where they had already begun to interact and in so doing had engendered a masterpiece.

However, in obedience to the national mores he went "Home" and set about putting the colonial episode behind him. He managed at length to get it out of sight, but never out of memory. "Home," it is probable, would have treated him a little less coldly had there been more graciousness on his part, but he lost ease faster than he gained it. As is not uncommon with bachelors and spinsters, be became militantly possessive and tended to exaggerate the importance of what was his own: Jones was *his* friend, therefore an altogether admirable and charming fellow; *his* body servant Alfred was unique; *his* conclusions about evolution or the Odyssey or Shakespeare's sonnets were the only ones that made sense. He tended also toward another trait of the self-centered—to compensate his failures with a façade, a brisk show of "happiness" for the benefit of both himself and others. This attitude, this façade, he could not readily have maintained in New Zealand, where there was no really convenient place to hide. Could it have been that part of his frustration lay in the fact that he was a backtrailer from the frontier—that having thrown away his chance to help shape a new culture, he must wanton his resources in mordant criticisms of the old? Moorhouse remained an ideal to the end; was he a symbol of the man Butler might himself have become?

The fates, however, had set other patterns for his life. Already *Erewhon* foreshadowed a series of writings in which he enlarged and formalized his ideas on evolution, prompted first by a fast-growing disillusion with Darwinism which later erupted into a protracted quarrel with Darwin and his whole school. *Life and Habit* (1877) argues for unbroken extension of personality, back of individual birth and beyond individual death—for the identity, in effect, of parent and offspring, and for heredity as a function of memory. Evolution in this view is the result of adaptation by organisms through their own conscious needs, however small and stretching over however long a time, in contradistinction to blind natural selection. "He wanted a view of life in which the diverse needs of man's nature should be harmonized, a world in which the struggle for self-knowledge and personal freedom should constitute not an act of rebellion but an inevitable growth, in harmony with natural and social laws."[4] The search for such a view led him at length to a re-examination and subsequent defense of a series of pre-Darwinians whose theories permitted at least some degree of purposiveness in evolutionary variations: Buffon, Erasmus Darwin, and Lamarck. These men and their theories he championed in *Evolution Old and New* (1879) and shortly afterward became engaged in a bitter contention with the aging Darwin. Time and the sifting of evidence have shown this to have been a misunderstanding between two preternaturally sensitive men, involving erroneous personal judgments and needless exasperations on both sides. *Luck or Cunning?* appeared in 1886, further elaborating the memory-heredity theory and still insisting upon the principle of design behind evolution.

There were other scientific writings, but these are the chief ones—books which Butler felt (not without some reason) the scientific world shrugged off, refusing to take the author seriously as either a lay critic of Darwinism or a worthy proponent of its Lamarckian alternatives. For the ruling caste of scientists, who of course were largely dedicated Darwinians, Butler felt a mounting aggravation of antagonism which he did not struggle to conceal. He did not fight altogether alone, for he had satiric allies of some power and pretension in Thomas Love Peacock (*Gryll Grange,* 1860) and W. H. Mallock (*The New Republic,* 1877, and *The New Paul and Virginia,* 1878), neither of whom cared a whit more for scientism than he did. But these writers used ridicule more largely than reason, fable more largely than irony. And although Butler could not associate himself directly with the church in the controversy between science and religion, he was essentially closer to the clergy than to the group that he suspected of conniving at elevating themselves into high priests of power. The image which he constructed of himself was that of the lone prophet.

The *Note-Books,* in a Butlerian way of speaking, tell us all and at the same time tell us nothing. But it is hard for one to avoid a final impression of his deep disappointment: "My days run through me as water through a sieve . . . I have squandered my life as a schoolboy squanders a tip." There is the masquerade of high disdain, the factitious accounting to cover up the embezzlement, the chronic unwillingness to concede any fundamental error of choice. True, he took "the fighting road rather than the hang-on-to-a-great-man road," somewhat through inner necessity, perhaps, but also through more or less accidental external circumstances. Darwin, to begin with, had been the great man *par excellence* to hang on to. Fame was the spur: he longed for a seat upon an intellectual throne; and obscurity—in the one spot on earth where one was under compulsion to struggle the hardest for notice—was fatally damning to a career that craved attention and had not the knack of catching and holding it. Surely his alleged lofty indifference to public opinion cannot be taken seriously. He is throwing dust at our eyes, but not much of it gets in.

In 1882 he wrote:

When I am dead, do not let people say of me that I suffered from mis-representation and neglect. I was neglected and misrepresented; very likely not half as much as I supposed but, nevertheless, to some extent neglected and misrepresented. I growl at this sometime but, if the question were seriously put to me whether I would go on as I am or become famous in my own lifetime, I have no hesitation about which I should prefer. I will willingly pay the few hundreds of pounds which the neglect of my works costs me in order to be let alone and not plagued by the people who would come round me if I were known. . . . The only two things I should greatly care about if I had more money are a few more country outings and a little more varied and better cooked food.[5]

To this he added, in 1895, "I have long since obtained everything that a reasonable man can wish for." But in 1899 the mood of uncertainty was uppermost again:

It will be noted that my public appears to be a declining one; I attribute this to the long course of practical boycott to which I have been subjected for so many years, or, if not boycott, of sneer, snarl and misrepresentation. I cannot help it, nor if the truth were known, am I at any pains to try to do so.[6]

If we could be sure he meant all this—that it is not just part of an official view which he wanted to bequeath to the public that neglected him—there would be need for fewer interpretations than we have had. But the fact is, we can extract no consistent view of the man from what he says about himself, except to note that the perversity in his published works, those volumes for which he totted up the profits and losses so meticulously, is apparent in the self-criticisms as well. The exasperating critic is likewise an exasperating autobiographer, for, like the water-stained manuscript of *A First Year,* much of Butler's work has to be read mirror-wise, and mirrors are not always to be trusted.

Butler wanted to live again, or to continue to live, in men's minds. And in all justice he does—in the dogged loyalty to freedom that may yet survive in the mind of the sort of person who reads something in

163

Erewhon and says to himself, "This is what I mean by what I think but haven't ever quite said for myself: I'm grateful to have it said for me here." There is in no one other of Butler's works the same openness, balance, and sense of power that we feel in *Erewhon*. The book was more than "the sound of a new voice," for the new voice had in it the resonance of a new land, of Moorhouse's speech at the railway opening. Moreover, it teemed with potential new points of departure, like a sea-mine ready to explode upon contact with any of its bristling triggers. Most of these ideas were already in the germ before Butler left New Zealand: a perception of the all-but-inevitable antagonisms between parents and children ("Birth Formulae" and "The World of the Unborn"); anticlericalism ("The Musical Banks"); the commonsense antipathy to overtheoretical education ("The Colleges of Unreason"); the mechanistic perils latent in Darwinism ("The Book of the Machines").

Erewhon came slowly, Butler tells us. Well it might, for into it he was packing willy-nilly most of the ideas that would concern him for the next twenty years. It is hard to believe that the opening chapters caused him much difficulty; it must have been the Colleges of Unreason, the Musical Banks, the World of the Unborn that came into shape less readily than the already well-sketched Book of the Machines. Public demand, for once, was on his side, with a flurry of utopian fiction about this time; half a dozen or more books of a similar stripe appeared in the late sixties or early seventies. But *Erewhon* was the newest voice of all.

Erewhon appealed to the public partly because of its very perversity in sporting with utopia, partly because (as Butler wrote to Fleay, July 2, 1872), it had "real stuff in it."[7] And yet, with all its spoofing, it held something for the utopians. Here was a land which many readers must easily have identified as New Zealand; to many Englishmen, New Zealand had been an Erewhon all along and was to continue so.

Mesopotamia, however, had been no utopia; and even in using the New Zealand setting Butler was still more concerned with mental topography than with physical. He built (or aggregated) the volume

164

around "The Book of the Machines," out of which was to emerge at length his settled hostility to Darwinism.

When I advocated the theory of the livingness, or quasi-livingness of machines, in the chapters of *Erewhon* of which all else that I have written on biological subjects is a development, I took care that people should see the position in its extreme form; the non-livingness of bodily organs is to the full as startling a paradox as the livingness of non-bodily ones, and we have a right to expect the fullest explicitness from those who advance it. Of course it must be borne in mind that a machine can only claim any appreciable aroma of livingness so long as it is in actual use. In *Erewhon* I did not think it necessary to insist on this, and did not, indeed, yet fully know what I was driving at.[8]

The upshot of this was, in Butler's view, at least, that the scientists wound up advocating in earnest what he had proposed in jest, after the fashion that some of the pious had embraced the arguments of *The Fair Haven*. But this was no laughing matter; the existence of mind itself was at stake. In "The Book of the Machines" consciousness was deduced out of matter by hocus-pocus and applied to automata. By the middle seventies the issue was becoming clearer: Huxley was already "trying to expell consciousness and sentience from any causative action in the working of the universe."[9]

The ensuing battle was an ironical recapitulation in reverse (an Erewhonian situation in itself) of the controversy over Darwinism that had been conducted in the Christchurch *Press*, with Butler now on the side, to speak broadly, of the "Savoyard" Bishop of Wellington. "In *Erewhon* I did not, . . . indeed, yet fully know what I was driving at." Indeed he did not!

So much of what followed *Erewhon* is implicit in the work itself that it is worth lingering to see how it came into being. Butler himself commented on the process at various times. *Unconscious Memory* offers the most extensive account, which along with other testimony gives us a reasonably coherent description of the mental processes behind the book. He began, he says, with the hypothesis of man as a mechanism—

"this being the strand of the knot that I could then pick at most easily."[10] Here he had taken the position from which he soon found it necessary to retreat—not without encouragement to do so; but while in this phase it was not difficult to reverse the formula and think of mechanisms as potential men. This, in fiction, already had been done, though not so thoroughly. Soon he was probing other facets of the subject: might not machines be regarded as supplementary limbs? These two views went into *Erewhon* as the platforms of opposing parties, but the subject was not to be thus exhausted. *The Fair Haven* intervened; then Butler returned to his pet idea and wrought still another modification—the hypothesis that limbs are machines which the organism itself has contrived for its convenience.

The part of *Erewhon* which argues that tools and machines are a kind of extension of ourselves is, like the earlier parts of "The Book of the Machines," of New Zealand vintage. The point need not be insisted on, but it might be argued that in primitive situations, where so much depends upon the simple tools used continually through life, a feeling for the tool as an extension of the man is quite natural and strong. Workmen become attached to a particular tool and will grieve over its loss almost as if it were part of them, and indeed they genuinely feel that it is. Such attachment to tools, such feeling of identity with them, is something not to be come by merely by taking thought; obligatory association with tools as part of any pioneering experience would help considerably in solidifying and strengthening such an idea as the *Press* essay "Lucubratio Ebria" puts forward. *Luck or Cunning?* returns to the idea of tool-as-extension with a good bit of resolution.

What else could New Zealand have taught a bio-philosopher? If observation of animal behavior at close quarters and over extended reaches of time can be of any service, surely then Butler's Mesopotamian associations with sheep and horses and bullocks ought to be remembered when we consider his scientific writings. We have his testimony that "bullocks" would remain written on his heart until he died; and from what is said in *A First Year* it seems inevitable that "sheep" must have been similarly inscribed. He knew these creatures by pressure of necessity. How much of *Unconscious Memory* or *Life and Habit* was grooved into him in New Zealand? No estimate can be made; partly perhaps because he learned his lessons so thoroughly in such an exacting school that they receded into his own subconscious; partly because he sustained a lifelong effort to avoid reference to his colonial years. In any event, his experiences in wild nature are seldom made use of in his books on evolution.

The repeated act of contrivance, of course, is what in Butler's view is to be called evolution—evolution through purposeful action, not chance. Here we begin to lose ourselves in the resultant fracas, with paleo-Darwinians and neo-Darwinians taking the stage vacated by the ancestral Erewhonians. Art and music continued to interest Butler, however, and there were *Alps and Sanctuaries, Ex Voto,* and the "dramatic cantata" *Narcissus.* Then for somewhat more than a decade he was busy with the *Life and Letters of Dr. Samuel Butler* and his Homeric studies, Shakespeare's sonnets coming in for side attention. Seemingly, he had moved out of the orbits of religious and scientific polemics into the equally unstable orbit of literary scholarship—but only seemingly. In *Erewhon Revisited* he came back not only to New Zealand and to Erewhon but to the old jousting field for one final encounter.

When one approaches *Erewhon Revisited* with the volumes against Darwin and the Darwinians in mind, what might otherwise seem an attack upon religion per se appears as an attack upon credulity, which for literary effect is given a religious frame. Among the notes made in preparation for *Erewhon Revisited* is one especially revealing in its preoccupation with the quarrels that seemingly—but again, only seemingly—had been laid in their graves:

Let automata increase in variety and ingenuity till at last they present so many of the phenomena of life that the religious world declares they were designed and created by God as an independent species. The scientific world, on the other hand, denies that there is any design in connection with them, and holds that if any slight variation happened to arise by which a fortuitous combination of atoms occurred which was more suitable for advertising purposes (the automata were chiefly used for advertising) it was seized upon and preserved by natural selection.[11]

Another one of the notes is similarly indicative:

> Another poor fellow may be floored for having written an article on a scientific subject without having made free enough use of the words "patiently" and "carefully," and for having shown too obvious signs of thinking for himself.[12]

Butler was re-employing, moreover, the tactical movement by which he had retreated out of open controversy into satiric fiction at the outset of his career: after the flurry attendant upon the first dialogue in *The Press* had come "Darwin Among the Machines" and the lucubrations of the "Mad Correspondent." Unconsciously enough, by doing all this he was adding still more to the "pretty roundness" of his literary career.

Butler had been at greater length unkind to the zealots of the great scientific credo of his day than he had been to Christian orthodoxy in *The Fair Haven* and *The Way of All Flesh*. And now what he had long been in the habit of saying about Huxley, Allen, Lankester, Romanes, and Charles Darwin himself, he transferred easily to Hanky— who, it is to be remembered, is as much professor as theologian, both in title and in mode of thought, in a day when academics were still accorded a measure of public respect. Just as, in Butler's view of the matter, Darwin had foisted upon the world the irrational conception that pure chance (luck) can be a system of evolutionary direction, the apparently inexplicable events of Higgs's disappearance from Erewhon had been blown up, like Higgs's balloon itself, into a windbag of rationalized supernaturalism. In *Luck or Cunning?* he even went so far as to compare Darwin with Pope Julius II, and there are other places at which he remarks on the similarities between religious and scientific orthodoxy. "Sunchildism" is simply anything dogmatic that can manage to impose itself upon public credulity; in this respect it is as much scientific as religious. Here, some of Butler's earlier words on science and religion (from *Life and Habit*) are worth considering:

It may well be we shall find we have escaped from one set of taskmasters to fall into the hands of others far more ruthless. The tyranny of the Church is light in comparison with that which future generations may have to undergo at the hands of the doctrinaires. The Church did uphold a grace of some sort as the *summum bonum,* in comparison with which all so-called earthly knowledge—knowledge, that is to say, which had not passed through so many people as to have become living and incarnate—was unimportant. Do what we may, we are still drawn to the unspoken teaching of her less introspective ages with a force which no falsehood could command. Her buildings, her music, her architecture, touch us as none other on the whole can do; when she speaks there are many of us who think that she denies the deeper truths of her own profounder mind, and unfortunately her tendency is now towards more rather than less introspection. The more she gives way to this—the more she becomes conscious of knowing—the less she will know. But still her ideal is grace.

The so-called man of science, on the other hand, seems now generally inclined to make light of all knowledge, save of the pioneer character. His ideal is in selfconscious knowledge. Let us have no more Lo, here, with the professor; he very rarely knows what he says he knows; no sooner has he misled the world for a sufficient time with a great flourish of trumpets than he is toppled over by one more plausible than himself. He is but medicine-man, augur, priest, in its latest development; useful it may be, but requiring to be well watched by those who value freedom. Wait till he has become more powerful, and note the vagaries which his conceit of knowledge will indulge in. The Church did not persecute while she was still weak.[13]

There are other motifs, of course. Furbank, comparing *Erewhon Revisited* with Lytton's *The Coming Race* and Morris' *News from Nowhere,* makes a point of a kind of juvenility in all three works—a "fantasy of innocent luxury."[14] Panky is a child dressed up as a Professor; George is a glorified Boy Scout, of the Lad school of literature, presented in the homeopathic style of writing Innocence into characterizations of young people. "In the world-made-easy of the child's charade, the adult characters have no dignity; they are relieved of the necessity of dignity, and feel the easier for it. The adult treated as a child—the theme which we have noticed in Lytton and in Butler—has clearly a fascination for both these writers."[15] It is not quite certain whether we should assign this effect (admittedly present in *Erewhon Revisited*) altogether to Butler's fascination with Innocence and to his "search for a son." May not part of the juvenile behavior be accounted for by the fact that the actors are involved in so unnatural a plot that they are given little opportunity to behave otherwise? May it not also be true that here, as in most other satires, the tendency of satire itself is to oversimplify character, sacrificing it to the demands either of plot or of principle?

The plot of *Erewhon Revisited* confronts the returning Higgs (as the erstwhile cadet of *Erewhon* is now known) with unforeseen complications. Drawn irresistibly back to Erewhon, after twenty years' absence he is still able to retrace his route through the riverbeds and mountains up to the statues and beyond, hoping to remain anonymous and merely satisfy his curiosity. He discovers, however—to his amazement and horror—that he has become a god, the Sunchild, through the misunderstood circumstances of his original escape from Erewhon. (He left in a balloon, which popular imagination rapidly transmogrified into a celestial chariot.) He discovers moreover that he has become a father; that the young royal ranger George, whom he meets near the pass, is his son by Yram, the jailer's daughter of *Erewhon*, now married to the mayor of the metropolis. Sunchildism is in the hands of a group of autocratic, dogmatic exploiters, the chief of whom is Professor Hanky. Butler contrives a series of coincidences through which Hanky unwittingly delivers himself into the power of Higgs and Yram at just the time Hanky is plotting to destroy Higgs, whose revelations would, of course, deflate Sunchildism. During the dedication ceremony for a new Sunchild temple, Higgs challenges Hanky, who has laid plans for such a contingency and attempts to have the stranger burned as a mad heretic. Matters are peaceably settled in private through a combination of compromise and concealment, and Higgs leaves Erewhon, which by now is rapidly becoming Europeanized. The book contains side chapters and occasional short passages of satirical thrust, but the action takes up by far the greater part. Structurally, thus, it is quite different from *Erewhon*, and tonally as well.

The plot would seem to revolve around Higgs, but the controlling figure is really Hanky, who embodies at once all the arrogance and fatuousness of Sunchildism. It is to explode Hanky, not to find a son, that the Sunchild has really returned; and the scene of the unmasking in the cathedral is planned as the emotional climax: "You lying hound —I am the Sunchild!" The drama is part physical, part intellectual.

If Butler had a mission—and there are those who would stoutly deny that he did—it was the defense of intelligence. Darwin's natural selection, he was convinced, "pitchforked mind out of the universe" and left things altogether to chance, to luck. Even to think this consistently was, Butler believed, the crowning heresy of heresies; but to make it the cornerstone of a system—when, by first postulates, system had already been denied!—was an insufferable affront. Thus, to base a religion—any religion, Christianity not excluded—upon inexplicable accident was no better or worse than to erect a scientific superstructure upon the same principle. Thought is *not* an accident, the universe is *not* mindless—this we find Butler saying over and over. And when Hanky is made to behave as he does, we have the one incarnate representative of Butler's opposition—much more truly so than in Theobald Pontifex, who, though monstrous, is still human, as are most of the Erewhonians. But not Hanky; a thoroughgoing Jesuit (as Panky is an unthoroughgoing ritualist),[16] Hanky is not to be taken lightly. He is the opportunist, willing to operate within any promising framework, be it political, religious, commercial, scientific, or what not. Dangerous demagogue that he is, however, he seems hardly more than a surface; he has no extensively projected scheme of control other than the perpetuation of his kind. From another habitué of the British Museum, Karl Marx, Butler could have received hints of a darker Hankyism that was to draw attention from satirists in the next generation when utopia was called into court.

In the uncomfortable process of becoming an apostate Darwinian, Butler became also an apostate utopian. Mechanism gave the Darwinians something they took to be a firm basis for control which was not long in extending itself to politics, as, for instance, in the design of the French social philosopher Comte for the ideal society to be ruled by experts. Moderation and common sense were not the ideals of the Comtists, for they believed firmly that perfection lay within striking distance for those with the resolution to strike. If Butler at times was stubborn, so were his opponents, and his suspicions that they were after power and prestige were not altogether groundless. So was he, perhaps, after a measure of prestige, at least, but not within the framework of what might easily have become Prussian absolutism. In his total opposition to the leading scientific figures of his time he therefore set himself against the sort of intellectual arrogance that all too quickly, given opportunity, may turn into dictatorship—whether of Church, or State, or school. Taken in this light, the Erewhon books may be read as an early counterthrust—virtually the earliest, except for Peacock— to the unwitting process by which science-technology has been hammered into the tightly clutched implement of the power state. Other satiric prophets were to point this out along the way—Mallock, Mark Twain, Wells (though partly a utopian himself)—until in Thomas Henry Huxley's grandson Aldous and in George Orwell the culmination of protest appeared. The mid-twentieth-century utopia is a dirge.

On the personal side, *Erewhon Revisited* shows us a mind somewhat softened and tolerant, at times even compassionate. An attempt at emotional realization competes with the satire as it never did in *Erewhon*—a competition that is not to the artistic advantage of the novel, perhaps, but of interest for new glimpses of "old Butler." The father-son relation is much dwelt upon, as critics have adequately pointed out. Not so much has been said of Yram, who, deserving critical attention at least as much as George, has received justice only at the hands of Mrs. Stillman. As the portrait of Aunt Alethea in *The Way of All Flesh* is to be associated with Miss Savage, so is that of Yram

172

in its intellectual phases. Yram is quick-witted and intuitive, sharp at conversation, decisive. All this and more Miss Savage was, and though the physical parallel is largely lacking, it seems pretty certain that in a stab of memory the "little lame lady" returns:

> The ghost of the lock that Yram had then given him rose from the dead, and smote him as with a whip across the face. On what dust-heap had it not been thrown how many long years ago? Then she had never forgotten him? to have been remembered all these years by such a woman as that, and never to have heeded it—never to have found out what she was though he had seen her day after day for months. Ah! but she was then still budding. That was no excuse. If a lovable woman—aye, or any woman—has loved a man, even though he cannot marry her, or even wish to do so, at any rate let him not forget her—and he had forgotten Yram as completely until the last few days, as though he had never seen her![17]

If George is Butler's idealization of the son he never had, Yram is the idealized mother: the spirit of Elizabeth Mary Ann Savage in a womanly form to correspond. Could the "incarnate bachelor" have resisted this?

Self-portraiture is also more evident than in *Erewhon*: much of the behavior and thinking of Higgs the Sunchild is strictly Butlerian, whereas that of Higgs the cadet in *Erewhon* is not. In order to create Higgs the Sunchild it was necessary to interpolate some traits of character not altogether evident in the hidebound young man who blundered into Erewhon. "Old Butler" was personally involved in *Erewhon Revisited*—not to the same degree as in *The Way of All Flesh*, to be sure, but markedly more so than in *Erewhon*. Read with all this in mind, *Erewhon Revisited* becomes a testament supplementary, and in not a few respects contradictory, to *The Way of All Flesh*.

If we write off *A First Year in Canterbury Settlement*, then there actually is to be seen a sort of "pretty roundness" about Butler's career —within the framework of his life, that is. But *The Way of All Flesh* was still to be published, and at best one does not find *Erewhon Revisited* the seminal volume that *Erewhon* was. In the sequel Butler's pioneering experience comes back to him (if in fact it ever had left him) in vivid terms:

> He lit his fire, made himself some tea, ate his cold mutton and biscuits, and lit his pipe, exactly as he had done twenty years before. There was the clear starlit sky, the rushing river, and the stunted trees on the mountainside; the woodhens cried, and the "more-pork" hooted out her two monotonous notes exactly as they had done years since; one moment, and time had so flown backwards that youth came bounding back to him with the return of his youth's surroundings; the next, and the intervening twenty years—most of them grim ones—rose up mockingly before him, and the buoyancy of hope yielded to the despondency of admitted failure. By and by buoyancy reasserted itself, and soothed by the peace and beauty of the night, he wrapped himself up in his blanket and dropped off into a dreamless slumber.[18]

But in this sequel, the details of Higgs's second journey to Erewhon are passed over quickly. What is presented is authentic but not much developed: the riverbed scenery, the vegetation, the high-country weather, the equipment carried. Appropriately, the re-creation of the journey is left for the son in Chapter 27. Here it is clear enough that the old associations are still fresh; that Butler was not short-cutting Higgs's journey through lack of retention.* We meet local terms like "new chum," "fresh," and "Southerly Burster," and the name of the horse-dealer—Baker—reminds us of John Holland Baker, as the name of the shepherd—Horace (or Harris) Taylor—may recall one or more of ten different squatter Taylors mentioned by Acland. The proclivities and appearances of South Island rivers are still keenly recalled, along with such details as the "not much fly-blown" rug and the unfor-

---

* Booth speaks similarly of the South Island high country: "How well I remember the whole trip [to the Lindis gold fields] with its beauty, its very contrasts no doubt helping to impress it upon the memory. Such scenes and incidents are difficult to forget, even if one would, and each and all are as distinct to my mind in almost every detail at this moment as if I had been with them only yesterday, instead of more than forty years ago."—*Five Years in New Zealand,* p. 63.

gettable *Phormium tenax*, New Zealand flax. The view from the Port Hills is still bright and clear.*

"I have a strong, but not an uncritical, liking for his [Butler's] books," says G. D. H. Cole, "but, at bottom, no great liking for the man who wrote them."[19] Cole speaks for a good many readers, no doubt, but those who would agree too readily with this judgment need to be reminded that there was more than one Samuel Butler, even more than one "Erewhon Butler." The Butler nobody likes was the one who lived not at Mesopotamia and in Christchurch but at 15 Clifford's Inn, eating himself up in an abortive career of painting and a spate of little-regarded philippics against Darwinism, not to mention a twenty-years' wrangle with his father. Almost the only tonic influence of his London life, that of Miss Savage, was limited during its operation and cut by her early death. Some few of his relatives he found tolerable, but his immediate family, impossible. Pauli became a burden that he could never have been in Christchurch, and the friendship with Festing Jones

---

* The full extent to which New Zealand responded to Butler's attentions is not yet known. There seem to have been no local reviews of *Erewhon*, though some may still be found. Writing to the Rev. F. G. Fleay in August, 1873, Butler said: "Mr. Justice Richmond in New Zealand has been evidently much taken with it [*Erewhon*], and has dwelt upon it in his charge to the Marlborough grand Jury. This is the most gratifying notice I have had." Shortly before and directly after Butler's death there was a flurry of interest in the colony: O. T. J. Alpers' review of *Erewhon Revisited,* which brought such a cordial letter; an obituary notice in *The Press* (some five weeks following his death); and a review by Professor Sale of *The Way of All Flesh,* also in *The Press* in November of the same year. Passing mention of Butler was made during the first decade of this century; then the fiftieth anniversary of *The Press* in May, 1911, brought notice of Butler and republication of "Darwin Among the Machines" and "Lucubratio Ebria." In 1912 came H. Festing Jones's query which resurrected the original dialogue on Darwinism and some of the correspondence associated with it. Alpers' *Cheerful Yesterdays* (1928) contains a chapter devoted to Butler, and historical attention begins around 1930, the year of L. G. D. Acland's *The Early Canterbury Runs.* After 1930 there is a fairly steady stream of interest, with contributions by John Pascoe, A. C. Brassington, and others. On the whole, Butler's fame in New Zealand grew no more rapidly than in England, and he is still more often praised than read and studied there.

appears to have developed largely as an antidote to insufferable loneliness.

Having once completed the transition from self-reliant squattership to self-contained existence as a London gentleman, what had Butler gained by coming "Home"? For friends like Moorhouse, Fitzgerald, Haast, and a score of others he was to substitute Pauli, Jones, Miss Savage, a few casual acquaintances, and (once a week, at a pound a week) "Madame" Lucie Dumas. He was so lonely, one is ready to believe, that he was reduced to taking notes on the conversation of his valet and his washerwoman. In place of ascending unknown saddles and discovering new passes, he crisscrossed Suburbia on Sunday excursions. For responsibility he gradually substituted idiosyncrasy, in just the way he had said the successful squatters drifted into drink. Even with his money, the great elixir, it was the same: the fortune he had won (and deserved to win) at Mesopotamia he abruptly, ashamedly, called home only to have it squandered by London speculators. Not even in ruin could he shake free of Pauli, and soon he was doling out regular sums to Festing Jones. If this is a picture of ease and comfort, what would it have taken to be called shabby? One recalls the iron words of Robert Frost:

> Better to go down dignified
> With boughten friendship at your side
> Than none at all. Provide, provide!

Instead of enlarging and deepening his capacities, London desiccated him, immured him. It so thoroughly enfeebled him that he needed to remind himself periodically how "happy" he was and to break for occasional relief back to the mountains—the well-tailored Alps of Italy. His most attractive and enduring books, *The Way of All Flesh* excepted, are those whose roots are outside England: the two *Erewhons, Alps and Sanctuaries, Ex Voto, The Authoress of the Odyssey.* The wonder is not that he became crotchety and routine-ridden but that any sweetness at all stayed in him. Yet it would be untrue to say that he did not bring it on himself, for most of what plagued him might have been avoided.

"Let it be a stand-up fight between ourselves and posterity to see whether it can get rid of us or no," says Dr. Gurgoyle in *Erewhon Revisited*. Posterity has certainly not rid itself of Butler, nor does it appear likely soon to do so. *Erewhon* is part of our intellectual heritage, and a jolly part it is. It came out of pioneering struggle and success, out of the uplands and mountain passes and out of native lore, out of long evenings of talk at the station and in town, out of squibs for the local paper to keep a hand in light writing—all marvelously transmuted yet still bearing the mint-marks of Mesopotamia and Christchurch. Perhaps it came to be true, toward the end, that he was "happier in the days of his white beard than he ever was when he had a black one,"[20] but the record of his colonial life does not reveal him as unhappy. On the contrary, New Zealand lived a powerful vicarious existence in him to the end of his days, and when he died there was a good deal more of it than "bullocks" still written on his heart.

Oh, wonderful! wonderful! so lonely and so solemn . . .

Documentary Notes on the Text

PART I

Young Butler: Emigration or Frustration?

1. E. M. Forster, "The Legacy of Samuel Butler," *Listener* (June 12, 1952), p. 956.

2. Malcolm Muggeridge, *The Earnest Atheist* (London, Eyre & Spottiswoode, 1936), p. 79.

3. Charlotte Godley, *Letters from Early New Zealand* (Christchurch, Whitcombe & Tombs, 1951), p. 233.

Mesopotamia

1. D. O. W. Hall, *The Squatters* (Wellington, Department of Internal Affairs, 1940), p. 10.

2. L. G. D. Acland, *The Early Canterbury Runs* (rev. ed., Christchurch, Whitcombe & Tombs, 1946), p. 11.

3. *Ibid.,* p. 13.

4. *Ibid.,* p. 17.

5. *Ibid.,* p. 20.

6. C. L. Innes, *Canterbury Sketches* (Christchurch, "Lyttelton Times" Office, 1879), pp. 83, 87.

7. Acland, *op. cit.,* p. 140.

8. *Ibid.*

9. Samuel Butler, *A First Year in Canterbury Settlement and Other Early Sketches* (London, J. Cape, 1923), p. 109.

179

10. *Ibid.,* p. 165.

11. *Ibid.,* p. 88.

12. *Ibid.,* p. 128.

13. *Ibid.*

14. *Ibid.,* p. 96.

15. *Ibid.,* p. 97.

16. *Ibid.,* p. 177.

17. *Ibid.,* pp. 100–101.

18. *Ibid.,* p. 111.

19. *Ibid.,* pp. 169–170.

20. *Ibid.,* p. 116.

21. *Ibid.,* pp. 125–126.

22. *Ibid.,* pp. 124–125.

23. *Times* (London), September 10, 1932.

24. Acland, *op. cit.,* p. 150.

25. *A First Year,* p. 147.

26. *Ibid.,* pp. 148–149.

27. R. B. Booth, *Five Years in New Zealand* (London, J. G. Hammond & Co., 1912), p. 33.

28. *Ibid.*

29. *A First Year,* p. 101.

30. *Ibid.,* p. 168.

31. Acland, *op. cit.,* pp. 318–319.

32. *A First Year,* p. 170.

33. *Ibid.,* p. 155.

34. Acland, *op. cit.,* p. 209.

35. *A First Year,* p. 137.

36. *Ibid.,* pp. 137–138.

37. H. Festing Jones, *Samuel Butler, . . . A Memoir* (London, Macmillan, 1919), Vol. II, p. 372. (Hereinafter referred to as *Memoir.*)

38. Samuel Butler, *Erewhon Revisited* (London, J. Cape, 1925), p. 58.

39. L. J. Kennaway, *Crusts* (London, Exeter, 1874), pp. 106–107.

40. *Ibid.,* p. 172.

41. *Ibid.,* p. 178.

42. Booth, *op. cit.,* p. 38.

43. Acland, *op. cit.,* p. 208.

44. Booth, *op. cit.,* pp. 38–39.

45. *A First Year,* pp. 113–114.

46. Mrs. R. S. Garnett, *Samuel Butler and His Family Relations* (New York, E. P. Dutton, 1926), pp. 159 ff.

47. Booth, *op. cit.,* p. 30.

48. *Ibid.,* p. 72.

49. *Ibid.,* p. 77.

50. *Ibid.,* p. 101.

51. Acland, *op. cit.,* p. 76.

52. *A First Year,* pp. 166–167.

53. Booth, *op. cit.,* p. 20.

54. *A First Year,* p. 167.

55. *Ibid.*

56. *Ibid.,* p. 119.

57. *Ibid.,* pp. 99–100.

58. *Ibid.,* p. 100.

59. Samuel Butler, *Note-Books* (London, A. C. Fifield, 1918), p. 21.

60. *Ibid.,* p. 83.

61. Acland, *op. cit.,* p. 317.

62. Thomas A. Scot (pseud.?), *Chowbokiana* (Bombay, n.p., 1875), p. 100.

63. Acland, *op. cit.,* pp. 278–279.

64. J. W. Davidson, "Butler in the Antipodes," *Listener* (July 3, 1952), p. 28.

65. Acland, *op. cit.*, p. 286.

66. Oliver Duff, *New Zealand Now* (2d ed., London, George Allen & Unwin, 1956), p. 36 n.

67. Kennaway, *op. cit.*, p. 93.

68. *Ibid.*

69. *Ibid.*, pp. 94–103. The poem is dated "N.Z. 1861."

Christchurch

1. Paul Elmer More, *Shelburne Essays, Eleventh Series* (Boston, Houghton Mifflin, 1921), pp. 190–191.

2. *Ibid.*, p. 173.

3. H. F. Wigram, *The Story of Christchurch* (Christchurch, Lyttelton Times Co., 1916), p. 25.

4. Johannes C. Andersen, *Old Christchurch* (Christchurch, Simpson & Williams, 1949), p. 403.

5. *Ibid.*, p. 105.

6. Wigram, *op. cit.*, p. 259.

7. *Ibid.*, p. 253.

8. Andersen, *op. cit.*, pp. 362, 364.

9. Wigram, *op. cit.*, pp. 92, 96.

10. From *Canterbury Rhymes*, 1860, quoted in *Centennial: Canterbury, New Zealand* (Christchurch, Canterbury Junior Chamber of Commerce, 1950), p. 28.

11. Wigram, *op. cit.*, p. 135.

12. H. Guthrie-Smith, *Tutira* (Edinburgh, Blackwood, 1921), p. 219.

13. Wigram, *op. cit.*, pp. 100–102.

14. Acland, *op. cit.*, p. 160.

15. *Ibid.*, p. 83.

16. *Ibid.*, p. 153.

17. *Ibid.*

18. Andersen, *op. cit.*, p. 301.

19. *Note-Books*, p. 364.

20. Included in *A First Year,* pp. 221–223.

21. Andersen, *op. cit.,* p. 246.

22. *The Press* (Christchurch, N.Z.), June 11, 1864.

23. Andersen, *op. cit.,* p. 306.

24. Samuel Butler, *Erewhon* (London, J. Cape, 1923), p. 203.

25. *Note-Books,* pp. 311–312.

26. Booth, *op. cit.,* p. 50.

27. Innes, *op. cit.,* pp. 47–48.

28. *Erewhon,* p. 203.

29. Jones, *Memoir,* Vol. II, p. 362. "Reeves" was William Reeves (1825–91) of the *Lyttelton Times,* father of the notable New Zealand statesman William Pember Reeves (1857–1932).

30. *The Press,* December 2, 1863.

31. *Lyttelton Times* (Lyttelton, N.Z.), December 3, 1863.

32. *The Press,* December 3, 1863.

33. *Ibid.*

34. Andersen, *op. cit.,* p. 194.

35. *Ibid.,* p. 300.

36. Wigram, *op. cit.,* p. 249.

37. Sidney J. Baker, *New Zealand Slang* (Christchurch, Whitcombe & Tombs, n.d.), p. 42.

38. Information supplied by Mr. A. C. Brassington, Christchurch, N.Z.

39. Innes, *op. cit.,* pp. 117–119, 120–121.

40. Wigram, *op. cit.,* p. 145.

41. Samuel Butler, *Alps and Sanctuaries* (London, J. Cape, 1924), p. 60.

42. *Times* (London), September 10, 1932.

43. *Alps and Sanctuaries,* p. 43.

44. Andersen, *op. cit.,* pp. 338 f.

45. *Ibid.,* p. 348.

PART II

The Press

1. Kennaway, *op. cit.,* p. 228.

2. Quoted in Wigram, *op. cit.,* p. 49.

3. Jones, *Memoir,* Vol. I, p. 152.

4. *A First Year,* p. 87.

5. Jones, *Memoir,* Vol. I, p. 124.

6. Samuel Butler, *Unconscious Memory* (London, J. Cape, 1924), p. 17.

7. Garnett, *op. cit.,* p. 56.

8. G. D. H. Cole, *Samuel Butler* (London, Longmans, Green, 1925), p. 15.

9. Clara G. Stillman, *Samuel Butler* (New York, Viking, 1932), p. 53.

Erewhon: *Geography*

1. H. J. Massingham, "Samuel Butler and New Zealand," *Geographical Magazine,* Vol. 3 (October, 1936), p. 398.

2. John Pascoe, *Unclimbed New Zealand* (2d ed., London, George Allen & Unwin, 1950), pp. 75–76.

3. *A First Year,* pp. 121–122.

4. *Ibid.,* pp. 103–104.

5. *Ibid.,* p. 113.

6. Pascoe, *op. cit.,* p. 206.

7. *Erewhon Revisited,* pp. 2–3.

8. *Ibid.,* p. 16.

9. Jones, *Memoir,* Vol. I, pp. 151–152.

10. *Erewhon,* pp. 4–5.

11. *Ibid.,* pp. 3–4.

12. *Times* (London), September 10, 1932.

13. John Holland Baker, *A Surveyor in New Zealand* (Christchurch, Whitcombe & Tombs, 1932), pp. 34–35.

14. *Ibid.,* p. 37.

15. *Ibid.*, p. 38.

16. *Ibid.*, p. 39.

17. *Erewhon*, p. 16.

18. Samuel Butler, *The Fair Haven* (London, J. Cape, 1923), p. 189.

19. *Erewhon Revisited*, p. 17.

20. J. H. Baker, *op. cit.*, p. 40.

21. *Erewhon Revisited*, pp. 91–92.

Erewhon: *Ethnology*

1. Philip Henderson, *Samuel Butler* (Bloomington, Indiana University Press, 1954), p. 55.

2. *A First Year*, p. 156.

3. Samuel Butler, *The Way of All Flesh* (London, J. Cape, 1925), p. 388.

4. *Alps and Sanctuaries*, p. 97.

5. Augustus Earle, *Narrative of a Nine Months Residence in New Zealand in 1827* (London, Longman, Rees, Orme, Brown, Green, & Longman, 1832), p. 26.

6. *Ibid.*, p. 52.

7. J. S. Polack, *New Zealand: Being a Narrative of Travels and Adventures* (London, R. Bentley, 1838), Vol. I, p. 125.

8. Arthur S. Thomson, *The Story of New Zealand* (London, J. Murray, 1859), p. 301.

9. Johannes C. Andersen, *Maori Place Names* (Wellington, Polynesian Society of New Zealand, 1942), p. 238.

10. William Brown, *New Zealand and Its Aborigines* (London, Smith, Elder & Co., 1851), p. 100.

11. *Ibid.*, p. 101.

12. *Erewhon*, p. 9.

13. George F. Angas, *Savage Life and Scenes in Australia and New Zealand* (London, Smith, Elder & Co., 1847), Vol. I, p. 306.

14. Polack, *op. cit.*, Vol. I, p. 92.

15. Michael Russell, *Polynesia: or, an Historical Account of the Principal Islands in the South Sea, including New Zealand* (Edinburgh, Edinburgh Cab-

inet Library, 1842), pp. 378–379. (Russell was Bishop of Glasgow and Galloway.)

16. Richard Taylor, *Te Ika a Maui; or, New Zealand and Its Inhabitants* (London, Wertheim and Macintosh, 1855), p. 11.

17. *Ibid.,* p. 8.

18. *Ibid.,* p. 189.

19. *Ibid.,* pp. 190–191.

20. *A First Year,* p. 238.

21. W. Tyrone Power, *Sketches in New Zealand* (London, n.p., 1849), pp. 145–146.

22. *Alps and Sanctuaries,* p. 97.

23. Taylor, *op. cit.,* p. 9.

24. *Erewhon,* p. 206.

25. Thomson, *op. cit.,* p. 105.

26. Earle, *op. cit.,* p. 193.

27. Edward Shortland, *The Southern Districts of New Zealand* (London, Plymouth, 1851), pp. 30–31.

28. An attempt was made to father this article on Mr. Alan C. Brassington, but he denies any connections with the "A.B." of *The Press,* a writer whose identity appears to be unknown.

29. *The Press,* March 31, 1863.

30. *Erewhon,* pp. 70–71.

31. The figures are from Acland, *op. cit.,* pp. 252, 288.

32. *The Press,* March 31, 1863.

33. *Ibid.,* April 16, 1864.

34. *Erewhon,* p. 238.

35. *Ibid.,* p. 239.

36. *Ibid.,* p. 237.

The Progeny of Erewhon

1. Wigram, *op. cit.,* p. 99.

2. Massingham, *op. cit.,* pp. 399–400.

Documentary Notes

3. Stillman, *op. cit.,* p. 11.

4. *Ibid.,* p. 127.

5. *Note-Books,* pp. 366–367.

6. *Ibid.,* p. 369.

7. Butler to Fleay, quoted in J. B. Fort, *Samuel Butler* (Bordeaux, J. Bière, 1935), p. 113.

8. Samuel Butler, *Luck or Cunning?* (London, J. Cape, 1924), p. 113.

9. *Ibid.,* p. 120.

10. *Unconscious Memory,* p. 16.

11. *Note-Books,* p. 289.

12. *Ibid.,* p. 291.

13. Samuel Butler, *Life and Habit* (London, J. Cape, 1923), pp. 34–35.

14. P. N. Furbank, *Samuel Butler* (Cambridge, Cambridge University Press, 1948), p. 85.

15. *Ibid.,* p. 94.

16. Fort, *op. cit.,* p. 291.

17. *Erewhon Revisited,* p. 216.

18. *Ibid.,* p. 17.

19. Cole, *op. cit.,* p. 42.

20. Stillman, *op. cit.,* p. 240.

APPENDICES

Reprinted here for the first time are four pieces that appeared in *The Press* (Christchurch, New Zealand) during 1863, the year of Samuel Butler's principal contributions to that newspaper. The first two, "Darwin and the Novelists" and "Letter from Nimmer Beschweift," supply additional links in a chain of correspondence already reprinted in the Shrewsbury Edition of Butler's works. These are not attributable to Butler with any certainty. The third item, however—"From Our Mad Correspondent"—in all probability is Butler's. Around the review of *A First Year in Canterbury Settlement* (Appendix D) there hangs a mystery; it can be assigned to Butler only on speculative grounds, but its importance in helping explain his later antipathy toward the book seems obvious enough. Typographical peculiarities (not numerous) have been retained.

The presence in New Zealand of several paintings by Butler seems of enough interest to justify a brief listing (Appendix E). Acknowledgment is due the Robert McDougall Art Gallery (Christchurch) and the Alexander Turnbull Library (Wellington) for special information concerning the pictures.

"DARWIN AND THE NOVELISTS"

(*The Press* [Christchurch], March 28, 1863)

There is nothing more curious than the manner in which the human mind runs for a succession of years upon particular topics. One of the topics of the day is that which has been raised by Darwin, of the relations existing between the physical nature of man and of the lower animals. Darwin has attempted to gather from a great mass of facts, that there has been a steady upward progress in the development of animal life, from the primary *cell* to the finished human being. No one accustomed to the processes of a rigid logic can accept Darwin's conclusions as *proven*. The utmost which that great writer—for his worst enemies must consider him a writer of the greatest calibre—has done, has been to clear out of his path the primary impossibility thought to stand in the way of the conclusions at which he wishes us to arrive. He may be said to have established the fact that animals do largely develop from age to age, and under different circumstances; and that the struggle for existence is in some measure the parent of varieties in form and faculties. This is a condition which had been already arrived at as regards vegetable life, where one plant has frequently been changed into another by careful cultivation under peculiar circumstances. But a thing is not necessarily true because it is possible, and there are objections to Darwin's theory, which must suggest themselves to every man, lying wholly outside the range of his reasoning. Such, for example, is that derived from *language*. No one can read that magnificent chapter in Max Müller's lectures, in which, at the close of the reasoning by which he traces language up to its earliest roots, he concludes that the absence of the power of speech creates a vast and impassable chasm between man and all other created beings—no one can recollect this firm opinion of so eminent a philosopher, without feeling that much has to be done to reconcile the conclusions of physiology with those of the new science of language, before Darwin's theory can be accepted.

Appendix A

It must, too, present itself as a strange illustration of the theory of progress by "natural selection," that man is one of the feeblest, physically speaking, of all animals,—far from capable of most endurance, and far from being the most powerful; and notwithstanding is the lord of all. Whatever arguments Darwin relies on must deal with these and similar difficulties before anything like a philosophical truth can be said to be established.

But whilst Darwin is trying, through accumulated facts, to throw light on the subtle mystery of animal life, and the organic elements which man possesses in common with the lower animals, the imaginative writers have not been idle on the same topic. Two books are before us, both wonderful in their way, and both attempting to depict by creatures of the imagination, the manner in which man may partake of the nature of the lower forms of animal life. Both are by American writers, although the idea is one presenting more charm to the German mind. The one is Hawthorne's "Transformation"; the other is Wendell Phillips' [an error for Oliver Wendell Holmes's] "Elsie Venner."

In the former in which life, especially artists' life, in Rome is most exquisitely pourtrayed, a character is introduced—Donatello, Count of Monti Bene, who is supposed to partake of the nature of the Faun of the Greek mythology. In the opening scene the party of artists amongst whom the story is laid, remark his singular likeness to the celebrated statue—the Faun of Praxitiles. His character is pourtrayed as resembling the gentle, joyous, unintellectual, and frisky being of classical romance, who, in the infancy of the world, roamed about the woods, sporting with fountain nymphs, and living on friendly terms with the coarse and ungainly Satyr. And, as the story goes, we find that there was a legend in his family of their original ancestors having been actually one of the long vanished race of Fauns, and how a trace of the original descent was witnessed about once in a century, by a reappearance in the offspring of the tender leaf-shaped ear, clothed with finest fur, which grows so naturally amongst the silken curls of [the] wonderful statue of the Grecian sculptor.

The intermixture of the animal and human nature is the idea so marvellously developed throughout the whole book; and the moral agency by which the human intellectual being absorbs the lower nature, is wrought out with wonderful skill and delicacy of treatment. So much so, that we rise from the book saying—If Darwin's theory be true, then the old Greeks were right:—it was through the phase of Fauns and Satyrs that man rose from the beasts of the field, and modern science after all but establishe[s] the fables of heathen mythology.

Appendix A

Elsie Venner is a girl who was born a few weeks after her mother had been bitten by a rattlesnake, and only a few weeks before she died of the wound. The nature of the serpent is supposed to have passed into and become blended with the nature of the woman, and the whole genius of the tale lies in the development of the character which is the result of such a strange accident. To attempt to express or describe in one crude sentence what a man of remarkable genius has slowly and gradually elaborated in a volume, would be impossible. Suffice it to say that in Elsie Venner it is not the physical conditions of the monstrous biformity which are most striking, but the modification of the moral being. Strange thoughts are suggested, and not altogether pleasantly, as to the nature and source of crime, and how far responsibility can attach, when the moral nature is modified or transformed by peculiar physical organization.

Appendix B

LETTER FROM "NIMMER BESCHWEIFT"

(*The Press* [Christchurch], April 2, 1863)

SIR,—The article in Saturday's "Press" on "Darwin and the Novelists," was a *treat,* and I, for one, wish you might be prevailed upon to favour the public, your readers, by yielding to them more of such gratification.

My more immediate object is to ask whether Darwin's great theory could not be adopted—without any inconsistency—to apply to the whole living creation *except man*; for we happen to know that man was created in a certain image—in one particular guise, and that he is specially distinguished above all animals. In this way the philosopher's scheme would be freed from the everlasting stumbling block of man being included. It is probably at the outset a mistake to rank man at all among the animals the author has to consider and discriminate. I venture to believe it is a scientific error terming him animal. But even were there no record of the manner of his origin, the fact of man being reasonable should at any rate raise a question whether the principle of natural selection is not wrongly referred to his body instead of his mind, which is the only mode of making Darwin's theory—however it might be strained—possible of application to human beings. We have some warrant in supposing a progressive and extending improvement from age to age *in men's minds,* that is to say, *in men,* since the "mind's the standard of the man," whereas we lack data as to any improvement in physical powers. Profane history appears to cover too short a period for affording ground for an opinion on the latter point. However, modern changes progress more rapidly, and in our present highly wrought civilisation we may better hope to witness some resulting change of man's conformation. For instance, we can expect to behold faces needing no razor, and hair "parting" of itself, at the side or over the brow according to one's sex. Possibly it has been already overlooked that a bow legged man is a native horse rider, and those with eyes oblique are creatures born to do two jobs at once.

This age chiefly longs to be able to fly, apparently; and Monsieur de

193

Groof, a mellowed man, I presume, is said to have accomplished already what forms the aspiration of so many. Why should we not expect to find ere long infant Ariels among us?

The fact of man being a creature with a mind affects the theory awkwardly in all aspects. If we shall be what we mostly would be, behold "quot homines, tot sententiae" bars the way; for although as a general thing power of flight be agreed to be desirable, yet when the fashion of the wings comes under debate, a stoppage immediately ensues, especially by reason of the ladies' *sententiae,* unless a compromise like a kiwi's is effected. Certainly, to judge by the paucity and retrogression of Quaker notions, the aspirations to have wings like a dove's would awake but feeble response.

It may be gravely doubted whether men were ever other than they are in form. I assume that the "principle of selection" relates to utility solely, and for that reason little weight seems due to the opinion of my Lord Monboddo's. Those animals only have the caudal appendage which travel prone along the ground, the appendage serving I opine as balance to facilitate making a turn. Indeed it would be no wonder to me if some acute inquirer observed that a mouse, for example, with its tail cut off, was at an immense disadvantage as compared with a mouse not so amputated. And this probable fact throws light on the motive of the farmer's wife who we all know, who "cut of their" (the mice's) "tails with a carving knife." However, what I seek to arrive at, is, that man being upright would really obtain no advantage from a prolongation behind. Why then, assume that he ever had any? The assumption that he wore it away by sitting, sounds too little likely to induce us to suppose its former presence merely for the sake of that assumption. For it will not hold equally with respect to Manx cats and many creatures in precisely the same predicament as ourselves, and who cannot by any one be believed to have sat their tails clean off. Nay, if it is to be yielded that men were once so graced, it becames fairly questionable whether the appendage did prolong the vertebrae at all. Nothing is without a cause; and surely the former fashion of queues in England ought to indicate something, and the mode in China to this very day. Believe me there must be more in a queue than meets the cursory eye or has hitherto been imagined. A sharp observation might be advisable when the records of the Celestial Empire become some day at length disclosed to barbarian scrutiny; but meanwhile I, apologizing for this long intrusion, must continue crediting myself as one

Nimmer Beschweift.

Christchurch, 30th March, 1863

"FROM OUR MAD CORRESPONDENT"

(*The Press* [Christchurch], September 15, 1863)

SIR—A former correspondent pointed out the danger which menaces the human race from the development of machinery. He showed that the machines were gaining ground upon us, and slowly but surely enslaving us, and he proposed what he conceived to be the only politic course, namely, the destruction of all machinery whatsoever. I read that letter, was at once struck with its obvious truth, and being for a time in some measure under the influence of panic, should (if I had not been restrained by philosophers of less logical but more practical intellect) have commenced a crusade against machinery which would have most probably ended fatally for myself. As it is I shall attempt no public onslaught on the machines, but am carrying on a fierce warfare against them within the circle of my own family. I allow my wife no thimble; no one in the house has a button to his name; all our clothing is of plaited tussocks, which we fasten by means of green flax passed through holes which we have bitten with our teeth. You would be charmed to see my eldest daughter's petticoat made upon this plan. I shut my hens up, and allow them no chance of getting lime; egg shells and birds' nests are machinery, and as such I protest against them. My wife insists that I should leave the house standing, and for family reasons I have consented to allow it to remain for six weeks longer, by which time all reasonable cause for anxiety will be over. As soon as this event has happened the house shall come down; there is abundance of fine shelter in the surrounding scrub.

I have been betrayed, sir, into these family details by the exhilaration which naturally *   *   *   *   *

Two months have elapsed since I began this letter, and the feelings with which the remainder of it will be dictated can be imagined, but not described. My wife with the baby and all her children have left me about a fortnight ago, and I have not the faintest clue to their whereabouts. I am distracted with contending emotions, amongst the most prominent of which is a burning hatred for the whole human race, which, by its insane devotion to the use of machinery, has bereft me of those treasures which alone rendered my life endurable. The immediate cause of the departure of my family I attribute to a misunderstanding. I found that my eldest daughter was still in the habit of making a clandestine use of hooks and eyes, and my wife persisted in fastening her baby tussocks* with pins. I protested strongly against this sacrifice of principle to convenience, and insisted on the immediate destruction of the enemies of human happiness. My wife and daughter with many tears complied, but on rising the next morning I could see nothing of my family; their five forms in the deep fern were all that was left me of my dearest treasures. Under these circumstances I have determined to go over to the enemy. I will henceforth consider the machines my friends, will enlist myself on their side, and devote the remainder of my life to their development and victory over men. It is in accordance with this plan that this letter and those which are intended to follow it will be written. It may be asked why should I write to the newspapers instead of to the machines themselves, why not summon a monster meeting of machines, place the steam engine in the chair, and hold a council of war? I answer, the time is not yet ripe for this; we are as yet compelled to use stratagems; and (as my friend the needle very acutely pointed out) our plan is to turn man's besotted enthusiasm to our own advantage, to make him develop us to the utmost, and find himself enslaved unawares. He shall rivet his own fetters. He is doing so rapidly now, and is such a[n] utter fool that the more he rivets them the better he is pleased.

My object is to do my humble share towards pointing out what is the ultimatum, the ne plus ultra of perfection in mechanized development. It is satisfactory to have an end in view, even though that end be so far off that only a Darwinian posterity can arrive at it. I therefore venture to suggest that we declare machinery and the general development of the human race to be well and effectually completed when—when—when—Like the woman in white, I had almost committed myself of my secret. Nay, this is telling too much. I must content myself with disclosing something less than the whole. I will give a great step, but not the last. We will say then that a considerable advance has been made in mechanical development, when all men, in all places, without any loss of time, are cognizant through their senses, of all that they desire to be cognizant of in all other places, at a low rate of charge, so that the back country squatter may hear his wool sold in

* We presume that the baby was dressed in plaited tussocks instead of linen. [EDITOR'S NOTE.]

London and deal with the buyer himself—may sit in his own chair in a back country hut and hear the performance of Israel in Ægypt at Exeter Hall—may taste an ice on the Rakaia, which he is paying for and receiving in the Italian opera house Covent garden. Multiply instance *ad libitum*— this is the grand annihilation of time and place which we are all striving for, and which in one small part we have been permitted to see actually realised.

Every step of progress has been accomplished by physical exertion under the direction of intellectual exertion. The human body is the medium between the human mind and external things. Mind cannot act upon matter but through the nearer or remoter agency of body. If a dog wants to eat a bone, he must use his teeth; if a man want[s] to beat the dog, he may use a stick, but he must hold the stick with his hands: mind cannot act upon matter except through the body. Some mind, with very little exertion of body, can exercise a great effect upon matter. A man who can write a cheque for £50,000 has a very powerful mind; the exertion is trifling, the effect considerable. Multiply instances *ad libitum,* and proceed to the argument, that as the human body is the exponent of the human mind, and an instrument without which no improvements in mechanical contrivances can be effected, all that tends to develope, cultivate, and keep in sound and healthy condition the human body, tends to improvement in mechanical contrivances.

But that as the human body can only act in obedience to the mind thereto belonging, the development of mind is an essential for the development of mechanical contrivances. In point of fact it is much more essential. But the human mind is only developed in one way, *i.e.,* by being placed under new circumstances; and it can only be placed under new circumstances through the body, and in one or other of these three ways, or by a compound of one or more, or all of them.

These ways are, travel, conversation, or reading. Each word being taken in its widest sense, *i.e.,* travel, including the smallest motion, and thus involving all experimental action, as well as the longest journey; conversation, including the unspoken language of the eye, or gesticulation; and reading, including the observation of the signs of the times that come before the eyes, the reading of an electrical telegraph message, &c.

If, then, we improve bodily condition, and add to the facilities of acquiring knowledge, development of mechanical contrivances is sure to follow, and with the development of mechanical contrivances improvement in bodily and mental condition advances also; and these things act and react upon each other, and so the huge world pendulum moves the hands forward round the dial plate of time. (Ahem!) Practically, then, what do we want here? A bridge over the Rakaia by all means. Whatever dams matter dams mind, for the one cannot travel without the other. True we can send the mind from here to China in an instant of time, but a passage taken upon these terms is hardly found to be effective except in ghost stories. Tack your mind on to a bit of matter, write a letter and send it by post, and the case is changed; but what dams the matter will dam the mind, therefore *"brigenda est* Rakaia."

Here lies the secret of the thing. A man can say coooo-ey, and he may be heard within a radius of half a mile or a mile: depend upon it man learnt to say coooo-ey a long time before he learnt to bottle coooo-ey—to cork coooo-ey up in an envelope with a seal and send the said coooo-ey to England. All books are a modification of bottled coooo-ey. Considerable modification, but modification none the less. The distance from coooo-ey to Pearson on the Creed is considerable, but it is bridgeable enough (so is the step between a camel and a pig). Footprints—old pieces of dung—feathers dropped, and so forth—why shepherds read them, mark them, learn them, and inwardly digest them to this hour. These are made unintentionally; but on a great white day—a day never now discoverable, yet never surpassed in splendour and great consequence for mankind—some naked savage, perhaps in extreme distress, conceived the idea of making an intentional track for himself with a premeditated purpose of attracting the attention of others of his kind. He wrote them a letter—possibly he printed his foot upon sand three times side by side, or may be he broke three boughs. There the letter lay till called for, and it was ill written enough; still no sooner was the idea conceived of making a mark with the express purpose of that mark being seen by others, than the culmination of the idea in the pyramids, hieroglyphics, Roman inscriptions, parchment, paper, letters, printing, newspapers, the penny-post, Mudie's library, the electric telegraph, and the Great Exhibition of 1862, follow as mere matters of course. The connection between these things is not immediately obvious, but a little thought will render the matter quite easy; for there is one great principle underlying them all, and that principle is increased facility for the action of mind upon mind. By the first faint intentional marks made for the purpose of attracting the attention of others, the range of the action of man upon man became extended beyond the range of sound and sight; up to this time sound and sight had limited the radius within which animals or men could communicate with their fellows—no other animal but man has hit upon the intentional tacking of its mind onto matter, and without this no intellectual development and consequently no material development, is possible. The next process was to extend the duration of the action—to fix it, to render it permanent—for which purpose a heap of stones would soon suggest itself. True, the letter must still lie still till called for, must be very illegible, and be directed simply "to those whom it may concern," but it lasts longer and the action of man upon man is extended in point of time. The pyramids culminate this phase of progress: it does not seem likely that this idea will ever be carried beyond them. The next stage, one which doubtless began long before the culmination of intentional track plan in the pyramids, was the development of hieroglyphics—by which it was intended that the track intentional should say not only "Here there have been men," but should also indicate what men, when, why, and what they did, possibly first effected roughly by arrangement of stones, a stone for each man and so forth. But when the notion had got as far as hieroglyphics the action of mind upon mind was increased indefinitely as regards accuracy; range of distance, range of time remain where they were—but accuracy was the great step here attained, and this developed itself into letters which were not more accurate but more decipherable. The next step was paper and parchment, or the inscription rendered portable. The letter need now no longer lie till called for—it may be sent; and so mind goes hither and thither on its travels, bottled up in postman's bags, and seeking a matrimonial alliance with other mind. Whatever has tended to promote this matrimonial alliance of mind with mind will be found to have been attended with material progress; and nothing has been found to be so real and permanent a parent of good solid material welfare, as those things which have increased the facilities for the interchange of thought, experience, and opinion. Some minds are barren, but most minds will in a sort of fashion breed after their kind, and some will be like Peleus and become parents of a son better than themselves.

It is in this light that we must regard the mariner's compass, the crusades, the fall of the Roman empire, and the reformation. None of these things knew what they were doing. The inventor of the mariner's compass never thought of mariners till after he had found that the magnetic needle always pointed to the north, and then he doubtless little saw what it would come to: we are pulled through the world backwards and only see what we have passed. Those who started the crusades little saw that the one real result of all that waste was the interchange of thought and opinion between the nations of Christendom. When the Roman empire fell, few perceived that the West was to be overspread with the ruins of the East, and that the ruins would grow and change the tone of thought all over Europe; that the minds of men who had been dead for fifteen hundred years would suddenly come to life, reassert themselves, and show their revived influence in the language, architecture, painting, laws, and customs of the world. This was not what was looked for, yet this it was that came. Letters had done their work: they had fixed mind and bottled it, corked it, labelled it, laid it in bins, or libraries if you like it better, and so time was annihilated as regards the action of mind upon mind. Hence the progress. What the reformation did was this—it afforded few fresh facilities for the interchange of opinion— but it gave freedom to form opinion, freedom to utter opinion—and a secure home for freedom has, in consequence of the reformation, been at last founded in this British empire. True the reformers meant nothing less; but in the economy of this world results do not depend upon motives; they depend upon the thing done, and laugh the motive to scorn.

So Mudie's library is an enormous power for the world's advancement. Humble beginning—very small knowledge of the upshot of the matter— still in mere infancy—the principle to be developed—intimately connected with the pyramids, crusades, reformation, and all the rest of it * * * *

Yours, &c.,
LUNATICUS.

P.S.—Of course you will see that the upshot of all this is, that the foundation of a public library and reading room is of the very highest importance for the welfare of the settlement.

P.S. 2—If any one sees my wife and children knocking about, please send them to the *Press* Office.

Appendix D

"A FIRST YEAR IN CANTERBURY SETTLEMENT"

(*The Press* [Christchurch], October 28, 1863)

We have received a copy of a little work entitled "A First Year in Canter-bury Settlement," by one Samuel Butler. Who Mr. Butler may be we have not the remotest conception; but we should in a friendly manner advise him henceforward to keep his first impressions in M.S. until they become more matured and better worth presenting to the public. The preface (which, to do Mr. Butler justice is not written by him, nor apparently with his knowl-edge) informs us that the "unbiased impressions of colonial life as they fall freshly on a young mind may not be wholly devoid of interest." From this passage we should be led to suppose that Mr. Butler who writes the book is not the same Mr. Butler as one who is tolerably well known as a sheep farmer in the Rangitata district. Mr. Butler must have passed the first blush of juvenility when he arrived in this colony, and though not yet in the sere and yellow leaf is at present no youngster, but the coincidence in the christian name is singular, and on perusing the book (which thank goodness is not long) the frequent allusion to the Rangitata district may justly seem suspicious. We can arrive at only one conclusion, and though we have no personal acquaintance with Mr. Butler himself, we confess to having expected better things than those with which he has furnished us in the book before us. The fact is that the work is one which ought never to have been published. It is crude and wholly destitute of method, the faults in style are numerous, and there is an abundance of those details which, though interesting enough to the family circle of the writer, and therefore well enough adapted for a M.S. letter, are excruciatingly tedious to the general reader, and ought never to be allowed to exceed that circle for which they were originally intended. We grant that it is very tempting to publish letters of friends that may reach us from a distant quarter, and which, read through the eyes of affection, may seem deserving of a larger circulation than they can obtain in M.S., but it must be remembered in the present regular Noachian deluge of literature that "of making books there

201

is no end," and that unless valid reasons can be shown for supposing that a book is actually demanded by the public, or would be demanded if its contents were known, it is far wiser to refrain from publishing one.

It is possible that these letters may be more palatable, or rather one degree less unpalatable in England than to colonial readers, inasmuch as they treat of things which in England are comparatively unknown: but the vein of glib self-satisfaction and thinly concealed conceit which runs through the whole volume must render it almost amusingly nauseous even to the most charitable reader, who, like ourselves, has not the honor of a personal acquaintance with Mr. Butler himself. We have no wish to wound the author's feelings; but if he is as great a simpleton as his book would represent him to be, we would advise him henceforward to keep not only his first but also his second and third impressions entirely for the perusal of his own acquaintance.

On one point the book may be, to a certain extent, commended: the writer has throughout spoken in favor of Canterbury, and even where he has given us a rap on the knuckles he has not been maliciously spiteful in doing so; the book will do the settlement no harm and the reader no good, and with this much comment we proceed to give a few extracts. The aspect of Port Lyttelton is thus described:—

January 27, 1860.—Oh the heat! the clear transparent atmosphere and the dust! How shall I describe everything—the little townlet, for I cannot call it town, nestling beneath the bare hills that we have been looking at so longingly all the morning—the scattered wooden boxes of houses, with ragged roods of scrubby ground between them—the tussocks of brown grass—the huge wide-leafed flax, with its now seedy stem, sometimes 15 or 16 feet high, luxuriant and tropical looking—the healthy, clear complexioned men, shaggy-bearded, rowdy-hatted, and independent, pictures of rude health and strength—the stores, supplying all heterogeneous commodities—the mountains, rising right behind the harbour to a height of over a thousand feet—the varied outline of the harbour now smooth and sleeping. Ah me! pleasant sights and fresh to sea-stricken eyes.

Mr. Butler then dined at the Mitre (how interesting to the public)! climbed the hill which he styles "volcanic, brown, and dry; with large intervals of crumbling soil, and then a stiff, wiry, uncompromising looking tussock of the very hardest grass; then perhaps a flax bush, or as we in England should say, a flax plant; then more crumbly brown clay soil, mixed with fine but dried up grass, and then more tussocks; volcanic rock everywhere cropping out, sometimes red and tolerably soft, sometimes black and abominably hard: there was an uncomfortable prickly looking shrub too which they call Irishman."

*   *   *   *   *   *   *   *   *

The view from the top stands thus:—

At last we near the top, and look down upon the plain, bounded by the distant Appennines, that run through the middle of the island. Near at hand, at the foot of the hill, we saw a few pretty little box-like houses, in trim pretty little gardens, stacks of corn and fields, a little river with a craft or two lying near a wharf, whilst the nearer country was squared into many-coloured fields. But after all the view was rather of the "long stare" description. There was a great extent of country, but very few objects to attract the eye and make it rest any while in any given direction. The mountains wanted outlines; they were not broken up into fine forms like the Carnavonshire mountains, but were rather a long, blue, lofty, even line, like the Jura from Geneva or the Berwyn from Shrewsbury. The plains, too, were lovely in coloring, but would have been wonderfully improved by an object or two a little nearer than the mountains. I must confess that the view, though undoubtedly fine, rather disappointed me. The one in the direction of the harbour was infinitely superior.

This may be allowed to be a fairly correct description of the scene as it must have then appeared, and it is satisfactory to reflect that the railway would now form a feature in the scene which could not be passed unnoticed. Then it was not only not begun, but there seemed great doubts whether it would be undertaken for years.

The author kept his ears open to the conversation of the people whom he met at the hotel where he stayed, and the following remarks are the result of his observation.

The all-engrossing topics seemed to be sheep, horses, dogs, cattle, English grasses, paddocks, bush, and so forth. From about seven o'clock in the evening till about twelve at night I cannot say that I heard much else. These were the exact things I wanted to hear about, and I listened till they had been repeated so many times over that I almost grew tired of the subject, and wished the conversation would turn to something else. A few expressions were not familiar to me. When we should say in England "Certainly not," it is here "No fear," or "Don't YOU believe it." When they want to answer in the affirmative they say "It is so," "It does so." The word "hum," too, without pronouncing the *u,* is in amusing requisition. I perceived that this stood either for assent, or doubt, or wonder, or a general expression of comprehension without compromising the hummer's own opinion, and indeed for a great many more things than these; in fact, if a man did not want to say anything at all he said "hum hum." It is a very good expression, and saves much trouble when its familiar use has been acquired. Beyond these trifles I noticed no Yankeeism, and the conversation was English in point of expression. I was rather startled at hearing one gentleman ask another whether he meant to wash this year, and receive the answer "No." I soon discovered that a person's sheep are himself. If his sheep are clean, he is clean. He does not wash his SHEEP before shearing, but HE washes; and, most marvellous of all, it is not his sheep that lamb down but he lambs down himself.

With these extracts, which are in good truth the very best we could find in the book, and which are almost the only ones against which no very reasonable exception can be taken, we conclude our notice of this volume. We retain it in our possession, and though we have no wish to hold it *in terrorem* over the author's head, and to threaten him with continued extracts from it, we warn him candidly that the next book he writes we shall treat with less leniency, unless he has digested his matter before printing it. For the present we will spare his feelings, and except we are very hard up for matter will print no more extracts.

Appendix E

PAINTINGS BY SAMUEL BUTLER LOCATED
IN NEW ZEALAND

1. Self-Portrait. Oil on canvas, 16½″ × 20¼. Robert McDougall Art Gallery, Christchurch. Signed "S. Butler Augt 1873." Presented to Canterbury by Butler's executors, through O. T. J. Alpers, who in a speech on August 24, 1908 (at the opening of the Annual Sketch Exhibition) assigned it to the Canterbury Society of Arts, stating that it belonged to Butler's student period and was reputed to be "a very striking likeness." Face, florid; lips, intense red; hair, dark-brown; coat, green-black; white collar; blackish-green background.

2. Self-Portrait. Oil on cardboard, 10″ × 12″. Alexander Turnbull Library, Wellington. Given to William Sefton Moorhouse by Butler (as were also Nos. 3 and 4, following), and—in 1942—to the Turnbull Library by William Du Bois Ferguson, nephew of Moorhouse. Flesh color, rosy olive; sky, light-blue, paling toward horizon; foreground dingy tan; background greenish-brown to light-yellowish, with a band of dull lightish crimson. In poor condition, with several blemishes. "The whole picture is nondescript, chiefly of interest in that it shows the younger Butler," says Mr. C. R. H. Taylor, the Turnbull librarian, in a letter to the author.

3. Portrait. Unidentified woman. Oil on cardboard, 10″ × 11 9/10″, seemingly a companion piece to the self-portrait described immediately above. Alexander Turnbull Library, Wellington. Sitter a woman in thirties or early forties, facing right, head half-face to the viewer; dark-chestnut hair, slightly heavy features with long nose and full lips, dark-blue eyes. Some damage, though not so much as to No. 2. Again quoting Mr. Taylor, "The portrait is not so wooden as the other, but lacks a very definite personality. Although very much better technically, it is probably also an early work."

4. Portrait. "Head of a Young Woman." Oil on canvas, 12″ × 14″. Signed and dated upper right, "S. Butler. 1860." Alexander Turnbull Library, Wellington. Decidedly the best of the three Turnbull items; a very

much more accomplished work and in all probability a much later one. Prominently displayed near a full glass-case of books and other Butleriana. Sitter a girl of seventeen to nineteen; close-up of head and shoulders shows head tilted to left, resting on right hand in a somewhat dreamy pose. Face full oval, done in warm rosy flesh-tints, with flowing dark-brown hair falling loosely on either side. Eyes brown; fairly full lips, high-lighted in light scarlet-crimson. Dress, a shadowed pale vieux-rose, apparently cotton; V-neck and deep collar frilled at bottom and tied in a bow with narrow ribbons. Background, midgreen toned with brown; slight shading of white. Cracking in circle below face and slight cracking in face have been treated to arrest deterioration.

5. Portrait. "John Marshman." Oil on canvas, 12″ × 14″. Signed "S. Butler 1866." Canterbury Arts Society, Christchurch. Clean-shaven young face with fresh complexion; dark eyes; thick dark-brown hair; standing white collar parted for chin; bulky bow tie; tie and coat nearly black. Gray background, flaking in places.

6. Portrait. "Thomas Cass." Oil on canvas, 16″ × 20½″. Signed "S. Butler 1868." Canterbury Museum. Head and shoulders; fresh complexion; gray beard, with hair above forehead dull-brown and dark-gray; black coat; dull-brown background.

7. Watercolor. English beach scene. Horizontal 6¼″ × 10¼″. Canterbury Museum, presented by H. G. Reeves.

8. Watercolor. Langar Rectory. Horizontal 7¼″ × 10⅜″. Spotted. Canterbury Museum, presented by H. G. Reeves.

INDEX

Richardson, E. (Australian contractor): 72

Richmond, Mr. Justice (of N.Z.): 175 n.

Rivers: of New Zealand, described, 23 f.; as boundaries, 27, 39

Roads: early New Zealand, 25

Rockwood (sheep station): 49

Rolleston, William (squatter-statesman): as bullock driver, 35; intellectual attainments of, 47; mentioned, 39, 49, 80, 85

Roman Emperor (ship): 15

Romanes, George John (Darwinian scientist): 168

Romans: compared with South Sea Islanders, 134, 140

Rowley, Thomas (squatter): 49

Royal College of Surgeons: 146

Royal Princess' Theatre (Christchurch): 67

Russell, Right Rev. M. (*Polynesia*): quoted, 140 f.

Russians: mentioned, 152

St. James (London church): Butler lay assistant at, 127

St. John's College, Cambridge: 7

Sale, George S. (squatter, editor, etc.): 39, 82, 175 n.

Satire (and satirists): on Butler, 54 ff.; Butler's, general, 56, 66, 82, 83–84, 140, 167–168; of Christchurch, 60–61, 63–64, 66–67, 68, 98, 105; in *Erewhon*, 94–95, 112–113, 116, 147, 150, 153–154, 156; in *The Press*, 98, 105 ff., 113, 140; influence of Maning upon Butler in, 150; Butler's, on English colonial policy, 153; allies of Butler, 162, 171–172; mentioned, 21, 172. See also *Erewhon*, Erewhonians, *Erewhon Revisited*

Saturday Review (London): quoted by Butler, 103

Savage, Elizabeth Mary Ann: influence on Butler, 94; compared with Yram of *Erewhon Revisited*, 172; mentioned, 175

"Savoyard, The" (writer in *The Press*): 103 f.

Scab: insect parasite on sheep, 20, 38 f.; fines for, parallel with *muru*, 149

Scenery: New Zealand, contrasted with European, 25; 115–131 *passim;* in *Erewhon Revisited*, 130; perfunctory description of, in *Erewhon* books, 131

Science: orthodoxy in, 168 f.; latent tyranny in, 169; dictatorship of, foreseen by Butler, 172

Science-technology: implement of the power state, 172

Scientists: as priests of power, 162

Servants: treatment of, in N.Z., 45

Sewell, Henry: on early Christchurch, 63, 64; account of early New Zealand dance, 86 f.

"Shagroons" (nickname for Australians in N.Z.): 18, 20

Shakespeare, William: 66, 136, 160

Shaw, George Bernard: mentioned, 158

Shearing: 40, 56, 98

Sheath, A.: speaker at railway opening, 78

Sheep: real masters of the run, 27; butchered, 32 f.; poisoned by *tutu*, 32 n.; care of, 34; mentioned, 166

Sheep country: paramount importance of, in N.Z., 41–42; as subject of conversation, 87; search for, in *Erewhon*, 125 f.; located by J. H. Baker, 126; exploration for, 128 f.

Sheep farmers: intellectual level of, 51